101 JUMPING EXERCISES
FOR HORSE & RIDER

Linda Allen on Mystic.

101 JUMPING EXERCISES
FOR HORSE & RIDER

LINDA L. ALLEN
WITH DIANNA R. DENNIS

Foreword by Olympic Gold Medalists
David O'Connor, Joe Fargis, and William Steinkraus

ILLUSTRATIONS BY SUSAN E. HARRIS

David & Charles

A DAVID & CHARLES BOOK

First published in the UK by David & Charles in 2003
Originally published in the USA by Storey Publishing, LLC

ISBN 0 7153 1707 5

Printed in Canada by Transcontinental
for David & Charles
Brunel House   Newton Abbot   Devon

Visit our website at www.davidandcharles.co.uk

David & Charles books are available from all good
bookshops; alternatively you can contact our Orderline on
(0)1626 334555 or write to us at FREEPOST EX2 110,
David & Charles Direct, Newton Abbot, TQ12 4ZZ (no stamp
required UK mainland).

Edited by Deborah Burns
Cover design by Rob Johnson, Johnson Design
Art direction by Meredith Maker
Text design by Susan Bernier
Text production by Kelley Nesbit
Copy-edited by Sue Ducharme

Front cover photograph © HorseSource/Peter Llewellyn
Back cover photograph courtesy of Linda Allen
Interior photographs: courtesy of Linda Allen, ii, v, xii, 8, 98, 146,
227; © Cathrine Cammett, 209; © Tony DeCosta, vi, 66; ©
HorseSource/Peter Llewellyn, 112, 168, 196; © Charles Mann, xi, 14;
© Tish Quirk, x, 13,122, 208; by Ed Lacey, courtesy of William
Steinkraus, viii; courtesy of James Wofford, 210
Illustrations by Susan E. Harris
Arena diagrams by Chuck Galey
Indexed by Susan Olason/Indexes & Knowledge Maps
Special thanks to Rodrigo Pessoa, pictured on the cover, for permission
to use this and other photographs, and to Missy Clark, Anthony
D'Ambrosio, Joe Fargis, Hap Hansen, David O'Connor, William
Steinkraus, and James Wofford for their contributions to this book.

Dedicated to our HORSES,
whose patience and
unique brand of intelligence
never cease to amaze us

And to the memory of Bert de Nemethy,
a true master of classical horsemanship

Grand Prix Show Jumper Peter Leone.

CONTENTS

William Steinkraus on Snowbound, winning the 1968 Olympic Gold Medal.

FOREWORD

Getting to Carnegie Hall

by William Steinkraus, 1968 Individual Olympic Gold Medal, Show Jumping

So how *do* you get to Carnegie Hall? We've all heard the punch line: *practice.* It's a provocative idea with an element of truth, but as we all also know, success is really not quite that simple. Another piece of the success puzzle would be, "Where are you starting from?" You'd also need to ask, "What should I practice — and how often, and for how long?"

In a general way, the basic answers to such questions are the same whether you aspire to play in Carnegie Hall or ride in the Olympic Games. What you have to practice, in order to fulfill your true potential, is everything you will need to master, from the most basic, simplest skills to the most difficult and complex. Even more important is the quality of practice: you have to practice correctly, not just go through the motions. But surely, the sounder your technical foundation and the more approaches to achieving your goal that you've mastered, the better you'll be able to accomplish any particular component when the time comes.

This book deals with the kinds of exercises you will need to master before you can think realistically about meeting the challenge of jumping obstacles, whatever their degree of difficulty or the complexity of their arrangement. When I was a kid in the 1930s, most of the courses we jumped weren't very complicated, and even the best horsemen didn't spend much time inventing fancy schooling exercises. We didn't have to. Today, however, it's a very different matter, for even Equitation courses can be *very* complicated and pose lots of technical questions. Any rider who hasn't worked out most of these problems in schooling wouldn't stand a chance.

I myself had never realized how much you could accomplish with cavalletti and gymnastic exercises until I came under the influence of Bertalan de Nemethy, the late, great trainer of the United States Equestrian Team (USET), and this may well have been Linda's experience, too. For surely one of the cornerstones of Bert's success — and that of his team — was the fact that horses and riders who had graduated from his comprehensive course of cavalletti and gymnastics rarely encountered on course a problem that they did not know how to solve and had not practiced solving over and over again, and in a variety of different ways. Bert surely knew a lot of different ways to get to Carnegie Hall, and as his pupils demonstrated, he knew how to build the technical foundation one requires to meet Show Jumping challenges, even at the Olympic level.

Linda Allen is a horsewoman of vast experience who has, since her retirement as a top-notch competitor, observed the best riders in the world on a very regular basis. As a world-class course designer, she has been the one to decide which questions to ask of Show Jumping's elite on many occasions. The schooling exercises she and her guest experts have set forth on the following pages are a marvelous and generous contribution to the sport of Show Jumping, for they can provide the foundation for solving even the knottiest problems today's best course designers typically pose.

Indeed, I'll be so bold as to say that if you can master all 101 of Linda's examples, you'll never encounter anything on a course that will surprise you — at least very much. I'll add that you shouldn't let the fact that Linda has offered such a comprehensive selection of exercises discourage you from modifying or amplifying them, or from inventing your own. But what she has done in this book is nothing less than to show you how to build a rock solid jumping technique, both for yourself and your horses. From there on, it's up to you!

The Equestrian Equation

by Joe Fargis, 1984 Individual Olympic Gold Medal, Show Jumping

Practice is just one part of the equestrian equation.

Partnership is another critical piece, a partnership developed through patience and practice. To build on Bill's musical metaphor, a rider is never a soloist, he is always part of a duet. Carnegie Hall isn't just a solo recital; there is an accompanist, a trio, a quartet, or even an orchestra to consider.

There can be no rider without the horse.

Cavalletti and gymnastic exercises from the ground up are the perfect way to develop your partnership with your horse. These exercises provide a framework for training and honing the skills of rider and horse both separately and together. They allow you to concentrate, "focus," on your and/or your horse's weaknesses and safely develop those into strengths.

I consider myself lucky to have started my International career toward the end of Bill's and still be successfully competing today. Our training was the same under the guidance of the late Bert de Nemethy: formal and informal use of cavalletti, the types of exercises Linda has included in this book. I believe my longevity and success as a rider can be attributed to plenty of patient practice over exercises such as these, which start at the beginning and create a solid foundation for horse and rider, then progress to the most complex questions that may be found on a jumping course today.

I have been fortunate to have known Linda through most of these years, first, as a competitor, then when she was Chef d'Equipe for our Nations Cup team at Spruce Meadows, and now as a top International/Olympic course designer. It has been a privilege to know her and to share some of my favorite exercises here.

Use this book to practice, and practice patiently; you will not only improve your show ring performance, you will increase your connection with, and appreciation of, your equine partner.

Joe Fargis on Touch of Class.

Two Minds Thinking as One

by David O'Connor, 2000 Individual Olympic Gold Medal, Eventing

Riding horses is like a highly complex puzzle that humans have been struggling to complete for the past three thousand years. No doubt the horse has flourished under human care in war, transportation, and farming, but it has often been at a terrible price. Now that those elements are unneeded in most of the world, the horse can turn to what he was probably looking for all along from humans: companionship, trust, and food. "Will work for food" is not just a cliché when it comes to horses.

Interspecies communication — especially in the partnership between horse and human — is never easy. It demands great in-depth soul-searching that can make us better social beings within our own species as well as constantly growing partners with our horses.

Jumping horses as a sport and a pastime has been around since the first child said, "Look, Dad, see what I can do!" Jumping has become a huge sport with worldwide attention and loyal fans. Being able to negotiate a complex series of questions is every jump rider's dream. To have your communication so fine-tuned that two minds seem to be thinking as one, is the nirvana of all equestrians.

I think of this challenge as the puzzle, and if I don't have all of the pieces, there is no way that I am ever going to be able to complete it, even if I am lucky. Creating those pieces is a constant goal for every partnership.

This book is about creating those parts in an infinite number of ways. Having those pieces and perfecting their use is the key not only to competitive success, but also to any horse-related activity. Ever see those 3-D puzzles where all of the different pieces are connected in some way, and if one of the pieces is missing the whole puzzle cannot be built? That is what competitive riding is like: building the communication and

creating all of the parts of the puzzle before your competition begins.

Linda's credibility in this field is unchallenged. From rider to trainer to Olympic course designer she has thought through and produced these pieces in a way that will be a great benefit to all.

Good luck with your riding. I hope that Linda's enormous effort will help you attain your goals, whatever they might be.

David O'Connor on Gilt Edge, winning the Rolex Three-Day Event in Lexington, Kentucky, in 2001.

Karen Cudmore on Hawkeye.

INTRODUCTION

Riding and jumping, like most other activities, are best learned by doing. Practice is as essential for riders as ongoing training is for horses, no matter their current level. The old adage "Practice makes perfect" works best when modified to say: "Perfect practice makes perfect."

Getting Started

This book is for riders and instructors alike. The exercises are fairly straightforward and can be used by horses and riders at every level of experience. Keep in mind that even the easiest exercise can be difficult to ride perfectly!

These exercises are designed to be used by:

▶ Pleasure riders who are simply looking for new ways to enjoy their horses. The ground pole exercises, even without any jumping, improve accuracy, security, balance, and control, while offering an easy and fun new aspect to riding in the arena.

▶ Riders who are totally new to jumping, feel the urge to try it, and wish to do so in a way that is simple, safe, sensible, and fun.

▶ Novice, intermediate, or advanced riders looking for an effective way to improve their basics, correct their weaknesses, or brush up their technique.

▶ Instructors seeking a variety of ways to help their students learn and have fun in the process.

▶ Trainers looking for a step-by-step system to introduce jumping to the horse and ideas for overcoming some of the challenges faced with horses at every stage of training.

▶ Experienced competition riders eager for a fresh perspective on achieving and maintaining the competitive edge of horse and rider alike.

The majority of these exercises are rider exercises. To be done correctly, they require that the rider be totally focused and aware of each and every step taken by the horse. They also require, and thus teach, the important skills of keeping your mind focused ahead of your horse; your movements quiet, controlled, and ever so slightly behind those of your horse; and your balance perfectly in sync with your horse.

Every one of these exercises emphasizes the dialog between rider and horse. They teach your horse proper balance and technique, making jumping easier so he will jump confidently at the upper limits of his natural abilities. The skills learned through these exercises will leave your horse adept at making any necessary adjustments to avoid bumping the poles and will encourage him to maintain a proper **bascule** (arc) over every jump. The gymnastic exercises (#26 through 40) in particular will also teach him to think for himself. All the exercises offer you, the rider, the opportunity to perfect your quiet, steady, and consistent aids, so your horse willingly listens to your requests and responds instantly.

Some of the later exercises tackle specific trouble spots encountered in training or correct particular shortcomings in a horse's jumping technique.

The real secret to improvement through these exercises lies in the *way* you ride them. By paying attention to the smallest details throughout each exercise, you will become an *aware* rider — one who feels what is happening at every moment and knows when and how to respond. Your training goal should be consistent and polished performances, with an attentive, confident, and happy horse.

Why Not Use Complete Courses for Practice at Home?

Courses ask questions. The more questions asked, the more difficult the questions, and the more quickly the questions are presented, the tougher a given course will be to execute faultlessly. The answers to virtually every kind of question asked in competition are contained in this series of exercises.

Just as in other learned activities (physical and cerebral), progression from novice to skillful rider is accomplished by understanding the questions and learning how to find the answers. Skill is your ability to answer questions correctly, consistently, and confidently — first simple questions one at a time, and then more and more complex ones, until even a complicated series in rapid sequence is within your capacity.

Exercises, first short and simple, then increasingly longer and more complex, allow you and your horse to focus on particular aspects of the whole. Practice until correct and effective execution of the basics becomes habit for you both. It is impossible to focus fully on multiple simultaneous tasks; some things must become so automatic that they are always a part of everything you do.

For jumping, two habits are essential to good results:

1. Basics: Secure position and balance must be automatic.

2. Focus: A conscious awareness of where you are, where you are going, and what is necessary to get you there must be your top priority every moment you are on course.

Keep It Simple!

Whether you are a beginner at jumping, an experienced rider with a green horse, or a World Champion/Gold Medallist, success depends on solid, no-frills basics!

▶ Straightness ▶ Rhythm
▶ Balance ▶ Impulsion

These four qualities apply just as much to rider as to horse. A crooked or out-of-balance rider cannot produce a straight and balanced horse. A rider unable to "hold the rhythm in her head" while riding is unlikely to produce consistent, smooth rounds. Impulsion is a forward quality the horse displays; creating it (or tempering it in a hot, nervous, or overly sensitive horse) is high on the rider's to-do list.

The early exercises look very simple. They can be more difficult to ride than you think. They hold the key to all jumping, if you take care to do them *correctly*. Perfectionism is a good trait when it is applied at the right time, and that is *at the beginning, while you are working on the easiest portions*. If you develop the habit of noticing every tiny detail in your execution of these basic exercises, you will have taken a giant step toward your goal.

Having a Problem?

Every rider and horse find some things more difficult than others. Even the most experienced make errors and encounter problems. When faced with a problem, you first need to ask yourself, "What exactly happened?" It is important to be specific in your answer: "refusal" doesn't say much about the way the jump didn't get jumped!

Then, "Why did it happen?" First, determine a single *primary* cause. For example, a refusal in the form of a **run-out** is a steering problem first and foremost.

Finally, "How can I change my ride to correct that cause of the problem?" Here, keeping it simple is essential; plan in advance the simplest

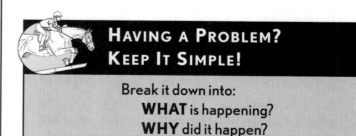

HAVING A PROBLEM?
KEEP IT SIMPLE!

Break it down into:
WHAT is happening?
WHY did it happen?
HOW do I fix it?

way to fix the single most likely reason that things went wrong.

In our run-out example, getting busy with your stick and spurs is useless for a steering problem. Concentrate on riding your approach so straight that your horse can't even consider going past the jump. If steering remains a problem, then you must return with renewed determination to the specific exercises that emphasize straightness.

Safety First

Minimizing risk is essential in any training program! Following a few simple rules can prevent most mishaps and mitigate the result should the unexpected happen.

First, always use proper equipment:

▶ **ASTM/SEI** approved safety helmets should be standard attire for all riders with good heads on their shoulders! When buying your helmet, always check the label, and take the trouble to find a good fit. Always replace your helmet whenever it receives a substantial blow. Safety helmets are designed like the bumpers on today's cars; they are effective because they work by crumpling on impact.

▶ **Shoes with heels** are crucial because the heel keeps your foot from getting caught in the stirrup in the event of a fall.

▶ **Body protectors** are now required to compete in Eventing as well as racing and could be an excellent addition to your safety gear when training. They can save your ribs and internal organs as well as your wind in case of a fall.

Second, always jump with someone in close proximity. As a matter of fact, even without jumping, it is wise to plan always to ride when someone is nearby. Accidents are rare but can happen just as easily over a cross rail or when

trotting around on the flat as over a 5-foot oxer. Why take the chance of a simple accident becoming a life-changing event?

SAFETY BASICS

▶ **Always wear an ASTM/SEI certified helmet**
▶ **Wear shoes with heels**
▶ **Never ride or jump alone**
▶ **Check your tack and equipment regularly**

Using a Trainer, Coach, Instructor, Ground Person, or Helper

It is far easier to progress with some help from the ground, in addition to being safer. A knowledgeable trainer or coach can simplify many things for you. When that is just not an option, however, you can still make good progress without a professional. Turn a helper into a "**ground person.**"

Your helper can be anyone willing to be a part of your training program — friend, sibling, spouse, parent, or another rider who is willing to trade their help for yours when they ride. While knowledge of horses is an advantage, even someone entirely new to the sport can quickly become a very helpful "pair of eyes" (and hands), sharing observations, videotaping, and even (especially!) learning to build the jumps. Having someone who can make the changes necessary to build the various exercises — add jumps, change heights, spreads, and distances — means you do not have to interrupt your training to dismount and do it yourself. Make your helper part of the process. You will both have fun and progress faster.

Your Arena, Jumps, and Other Equipment

These exercises can be built in a variety of settings, although a level area of a moderate size makes setting up and riding them easier. Less experienced riders should jump in an area enclosed by a fence.

A workable size for an outdoor jumping arena can range from 100 to 200 feet (30 to 60m) wide, with a length of 200 to 300 feet (60 to 100m). While a small arena may limit the complexity of the gymnastics you can set, many valuable patterns can be used in a very small space.

The surface should be even, provide some "cushion," and be neither slippery nor excessively deep.

Take the time to inspect your arena and equipment for rocks, protruding nails, large splinters, or any piece of equipment that a horse could put his foot through. Do not allow extra jump cups or pins to remain lying on the ground or empty on the standards. Horses or riders can get hurt by stepping on or bumping them. Why miss riding time with an avoidable bruise or cut?

Poles

All of the exercises make extensive use of poles. The best poles are between 3 and 4 inches (approx. 10cm) in diameter, 10 or 12 feet (3 or 4m) in length, and "machined" to a round shape. Almost every area has a lumber supplier that can obtain poles of this description. Octagonal poles, made from 4x4s, are a far less satisfactory substitute for machined versions, since the original lumber seldom has a straight enough grain to prevent frequent breakage.

Shorter poles are lighter to handle and fit more easily in small or indoor arenas. They require greater accuracy when riding the more complex exercises. Many top riders use shorter poles and simple stick **standards** (ones without wings) by choice when training — which makes the wider fences encountered in competition seem easier.

Cavalletti (poles raised from 2 to 10 inches [5 to 25cm] off the ground) are desirable under certain circumstances. They require a horse to *use himself*: that is, to round his back and bend his joints to a far greater degree than does a simple pole on the ground. If your aim is increased fitness, power, and concentration from your horse, it is worth the effort to raise the ground poles once you and your horse are comfortable riding an exercise with the poles on the ground.

A flat plank or a raised, semi-fixed cavalletti is a good replacement for a loose ground pole whenever a placing pole is called for immediately on the landing side of a jump.

Permanent trot cavallettis consisting of railroad ties or other heavy timber are wonderful to have if you have the space for them. Set four to six railroad ties evenly spaced for trot work, in a location to be approached from either direction. A spacing of 4 ft., 6 in. to 4 ft., 9 in. (1.4 to 1.5m) will be ideal for most horses.

While PVC poles are not the best for jumping, 4-inch plastic drainpipe (the non-shattering type) can be useful to have on hand for "guide" poles to keep your horse straight. In addition to being inexpensive, they are very light and easy to move. They can also serve as ground poles, but sensitive (hotter) horses tend to become upset

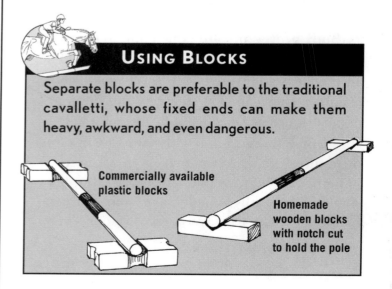

USING BLOCKS

Separate blocks are preferable to the traditional cavalletti, whose fixed ends can make them heavy, awkward, and even dangerous.

Commercially available plastic blocks

Homemade wooden blocks with notch cut to hold the pole

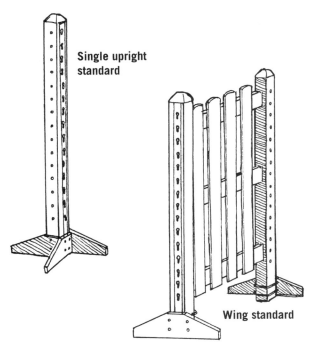

Single upright standard

Wing standard

These standards show both the "cup and pin" and "keyhole" systems for holding the rails.

over the sound and movement when PVC poles are bumped.

Other Jump Equipment

Plastic pylons are useful for marking turning points or delineating the various patterns. If orange cones (similar to those used in areas of road construction) are not readily available, plastic water buckets or some of your extra blocks can work just as well.

Simple, easy-to-modify equipment is best when constructing these exercises. A useful inventory includes an assortment of good jump poles (minimum of 12 rails, preferably closer to 50), 10 or 12 blocks (available either commer-

cially or homemade from short, notched sections of 6x8-inch [15.2 x 20.3cm] wood, which can be used to raise your poles when desired), and at least 10 (preferably 30 or 40) upright or wing standards.

Bits, Martingales, and Other Equipment

When it comes to bits, less is best. Spend time educating your horse; it is the only way to achieve lasting results.

While there can be good reasons for using special bits in competition, the least severe bit possible should be used while schooling. A plain snaffle is always the first choice, whether it be a medium thickness, hollow, rubber, or Bristol mouthpiece; full-cheek, round-ring, or D-ring. This type of training is meant to focus your horse's attention on your commands — a sharp bit will only discourage the kind of cooperation you want.

Martingales are optional. For a young horse with a tendency to toss his head up when playing, using a medium-length standing martingale might be a good idea. Running martingales are seldom needed when schooling simple exercises, although they might be helpful when jumping longer courses.

Draw reins for jumping, except in the hands of some exceptionally talented professional riders, are likely to compound problems rather than correct them. Although they can be useful for flatwork, they shouldn't be used for jumping unless you are under the supervision of an experienced trainer.

Boots or polo wraps, while optional, can prevent a slip during a turn or other misstep from resulting in a scratch or bruise.

How Is Your Position?

When it comes to position, "Beauty is as beauty does." Achieving solid and effective basics is the only way for both you and your horse to perform your best.

Often, flaws in position are overlooked until problems arise in a later stage of training. If your leg slips back, you could jump a simple cross bar, but over a bigger oxer, that slipped leg will leave you downright insecure. Your loose leg may be okay all summer on your quiet horse, but then one chilly fall morning, a playful buck at a critical moment might put you on the ground.

Use the exercises throughout this book to help figure out what you're doing right and what you're doing wrong. The basic ones provide the opportunity to fix weaknesses in your position. Ignore position or allow bad habits to persist, and your results will suffer over complete courses or higher jumps.

Correct leg position

Position consists of the following three essentials:

➤ **Secure.** This means being able to stay in the center of your horse, hands independent and body balanced, with a solid leg and base, and sufficient, relaxed flexibility to remain centered in your tack, even when your horse makes an unexpected move.

➤ **Effective.** The position and use of your legs, seat, upper body, arms, and hands should create the partnership with your horse that produces consistently good performances. Especially when jumping, "getting the job done" is much more than just looking pretty!

➤ **Adaptable.** An effective position permits a light seat, a two-point (or galloping) position, or a deeper, full seat. Jumping courses can require a rider to utilize each of these, depending on the

Incorrect leg in front

Incorrect leg behind

particular task at hand. The ability to move easily and naturally among the various seats, along with an understanding of when each is appropriate, is essential.

Key to a good position is a solid leg. The better your leg, the better your balance, and the more effective you will be over jumps. If you encounter problems, keep in mind that difficulties with your upper body are almost always a reflection of an incorrect or inconsistent leg position. Always remember: "Fix the leg first."

The most serious faults in leg position are:
➤ A thigh rotated out, placing the back of the knee in contact with the saddle;

➤ A braced knee, creating stiffness and rigidity in the other joints as well;

➤ A pinched knee, creating a "pivoting" lower leg and preventing the consistent, even contact from thigh to mid-calf that is most effective;

➤ Bracing the toe or ball of the foot against the stirrup rather than allowing the weight to flow through the stirrup into a deep and flexed heel. This deep heel provides the low balance point that is the mark of successful jumping riders.

HEELS AND KNEES

Note: Any rider having trouble getting her heels down first needs to be sure her knee is not "pinched." Relaxing the knee is necessary in order to permit the leg to lengthen down into the stirrup through a supple ankle, all the way down into the heel.

Three Basic Seats

Depending on the objective, riding over jumps requires three basic seats, referred to in this text as: full seat, light seat, and two-point (which you will sometimes hear described as galloping position or half-seat).

➤ **Light seat.** This is the basic and most frequently used position for jumping. Your weight is distributed primarily into your leg, sinking through supple hips, knees, and ankles, into your heel, while your seat (the front portion of your "seat bones," actually) maintains a light contact

Light seat

with the saddle. This position is appropriate for most schooling throughout the exercises in this book. A correct light seat with a medium stirrup length allows you to transition into a two-point or full seat instantly and naturally anytime these might be required.

➤ **Full seat.** Here the weight of your upper body is supported in the saddle through a supple yet straight and nearly vertical back. This position is seldom used when actually jumping. Its primary use is during those infrequent moments when every driving aid is essential, or when your horse needs the balance it can provide, around a slippery corner, for example. The ultimate use of the full seat is in

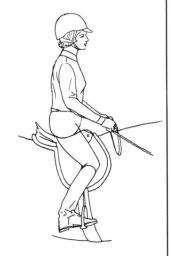

Full seat

pure dressage. The longer stirrup length and vertical upper body positioned directly over your seat bones, necessary for a full seat, are a hindrance when you must also accommodate the jumping efforts of your horse.

➤ **Two-point, half-seat, or galloping position.** This position puts 100 percent of your weight into your leg, permitting you to keep your seat entirely clear of the saddle. It is used when your horse will benefit from total noninterference from your seat. It is also an excellent exercise for strengthening your leg. Most riders find that Show Jumping over larger fences requires a somewhat shorter stirrup length than they use for flatwork and schooling over lower jumps. The most extreme example of short stirrup length is used by flat-racing jockeys, followed by steeplechase jockeys. Eventers on their Cross-country courses usually ride medium short.

Two-point position

Determining your own most suitable medium stirrup length will depend on your body type and degree of flexibility, coupled with the size and shape of your horse. Adjust to find a length that will permit you to sit and ride in a position as close to that shown in the illustration as possible.

The ability to use the aids independently and appropriately is critical to being an effective jumping rider. A rider who makes a habit of "clashing her aids" (kicking while tugging on the reins, for example) makes life miserable for the horse. Clashing aids will create a horse that refuses frequently or becomes hot and bothered by the very idea of jumping.

Here is a checklist of things you should be able to accomplish comfortably. Even if you are a real novice, you can proceed with the easier exercises; they will aid your progress. Wait until your position is secure before jumping higher. Fix any of the following problems before you tackle a "real" jump. The early exercises provide an effective and fun way to monitor your progress as you strengthen your position.

1. Can you hold a relaxed and balanced two-point position for at least two complete circuits of your arena, without leaning heavily on your hands, locking your knees, or letting your legs slip forward or back?

2. Can you sit the trot confidently and effectively, with a relaxed seat and hands that don't bounce?

3. Can you maintain a light or full-seat at the canter as well as canter in two-point?

4. Are your legs still and not kicking when you post the trot?

5. Is your upper body quiet, neither "pumping" nor "bouncing" at the canter?

6. Do your hands remain quiet at all times, and have you mastered smoothly shortening your reins at all gaits without bothering your horse?

7. Are you sure of your diagonals and leads, and can you feel which you are on without looking?

It is far better to wait until your position is secure before tackling higher jumps. Even if you are a real novice, however, you can proceed with the easier exercises. They will help you achieve all the goals mentioned above. The earlier exercises provide an effective and fun way to monitor your progress as you strengthen your position and master many of the basics you will need when riding over a course of jumps.

Linda Allen on Mystic.

Using This Book

Terms and Format

Most of the terms used here are explained throughout the text. Specific ones requiring basic definition are found in the glossary. When listed terms first appear in the text they are indicated in **bold**.

You will find directions for setting up and riding each exercise, as well as Hints, Problem-solving, Reminders, and "Doublecheck," which includes questions to ask yourself about your riding. Critical information and concepts are boxed. Each exercise includes a setup diagram.

Setting Up the Exercises

This book is intended to meet the needs of a wide variety of horses and riders. Thus, it is inappropriate to specify one "correct" height or exact distance for many of the exercises. Following are some general guidelines.

Jump Dimensions

As you determine the height and width of jumps, keep in mind the present level of training and experience of both you and your horse. Throughout this book, the text will describe the appropriate size for the obstacles as "small," "moderate," or "challenging."

You may interpret these terms as follows:

▶ "Small" is an obstacle that neither you nor your horse considers particularly difficult to manage, even under new circumstances or if you make a mistake in your approach or take-off. Generally, this will be in the range of 2 to 3 feet in height (60 to 90cm). If you are very new to jumping, the jumps can be even lower. Top riders recognize that they can accomplish valuable training over very small jumps when used correctly. The bonus is the negligible physical toll these small obstacles take on your horse. This allows you to use extensive repetition — the most effective educational tool with horses — to create good habits without injury or undue stress.

▶ "Moderate" indicates an obstacle constructed to somewhat larger dimensions. You should be totally comfortable jumping these obstacles, but they should be large enough to command your full attention.

▶ "Challenging" is used in places where you should raise your sights a bit, proving to your horse and yourself that the size of the jump is but one factor in a complex equation.

According to master horseman and jumping rider Gene Lewis, "If you always ride to small jumps *as though they were large*, you will not have to change a thing when the height goes up."

Distances

Since one rider might be training a small pony and another a 17·2-hand ex-racehorse, you should be prepared to take the "average" distances indicated and adjust them somewhat. The important thing is to produce the result that is described with your horse or pony. As you proceed into the exercises, you will find discussions of various distance issues, such as how to evaluate your particular horse's stride, and how your gait approaching a jump or the shape of the jumps affects the way you ride them. Adapt the range of distances indicated to suit your own horse's abilities and current level of training.

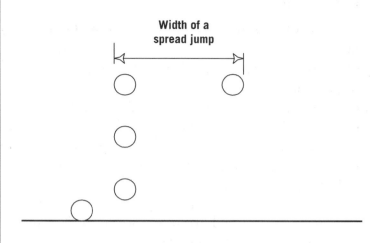

Width of a spread jump

The width of spread jumps is measured "outside to outside" of the top poles.

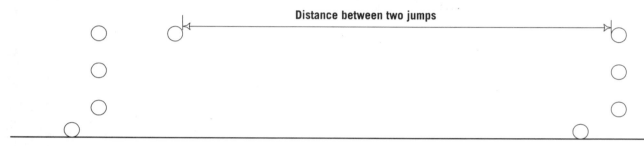

Distance between two jumps

The distance between any two obstacles is always measured according to the inner measurement between the jumps (from the back of the first obstacle to the front of the next). Disregard the position of ground lines for purposes of this measurement.

LENGTH OF STRIDE

Strides are the way you and your horse accommodate the distances between related fences on jumping courses. The ability to adjust his stride allows your horse to avoid taking an awkward jump when a fence comes up off-stride. Clever, experienced horses can adjust their stride so easily (and often invisibly) that they make almost any distance work out well.

Cross Poles (Cross Bars)

Construct cross poles so as to leave approximately 4 in. (10cm) between the two poles where they cross. This prevents the front pole from jamming against the back pole should a horse make a mistake and hit the jump solidly.

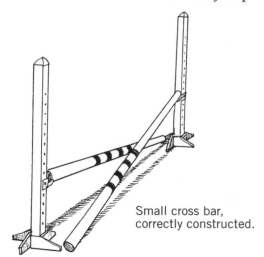

Small cross bar, correctly constructed.

Extra Poles

The addition of a second pole below the top one for vertical jumps (or for the front element of oxers) is recommended when the jump is higher than about 3 ft. (90cm). This becomes essential, for safety reasons, when the height exceeds 4 ft., 3 in. (1.3m). Avoid placing extra poles under the top pole on the *back* of an oxer unless the exercise calls for jumping the spread in both directions. In those cases, always leave a gap between the top pole and the pole below it of 12 in. (30cm), and avoid ground lines that are more than 6 in. (15cm) out from the jump on either side.

Ground Lines

Ground lines for the jumps are generally advisable when constructing these exercises. They encourage less experienced horses to jump in better form and help mitigate rider error. A pole or small flower box placed under or in front of your jump's front pole creates a nice ground line for training purposes. When placed in front, it is generally best to keep the distance between 6 and 20 in. (15 to 50cm). Some exceptions to this general rule of thumb are specifically mentioned, especially in the Challenges section.

VARIOUS TYPES OF GROUND LINES

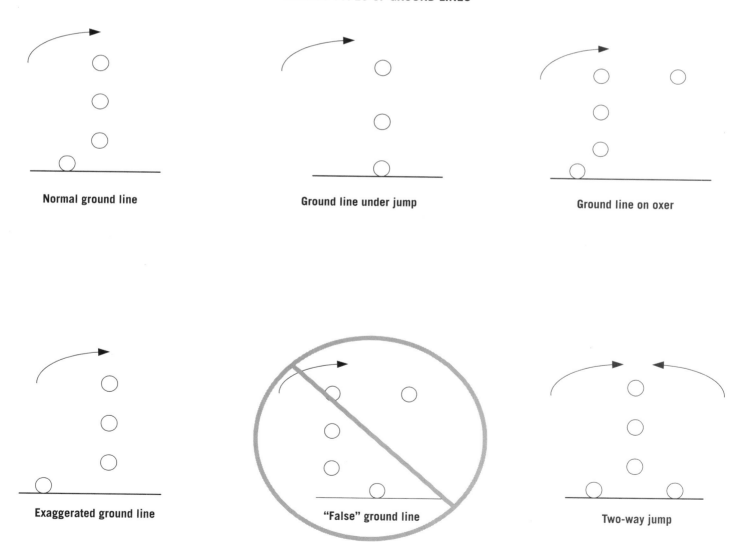

Normal ground line

Ground line under jump

Ground line on oxer

Exaggerated ground line

"False" ground line

Two-way jump

Safety Cups

Use FEI-certified safety cups to hold the back element of any spread jump when training. In the absence of safety cups, use the shallowest (nearly flat) jump cups available. A back rail set too snugly in cups can inflict punishment on tender equine shins for even a slight misjudgment on your horse's part and could result in loss of balance or even a fall. If shallow or safety cups are not available, have your helper place one end of the back pole on the back "lip" of the cup. (See illustration "Lipping the cup" on page 77.) Far better to ask your helper to pick up the pole occasionally than to have you or your horse suffer an avoidable accident.

SAFETY CUPS

Safety cups, first developed in 1993, are mandatory in competitions sanctioned by the Fédération Equestre Internationale (FEI). They are designed and carefully manufactured to "release" allowing the pole to fall free when a horse delivers approximately 135 kilos of downward pressure. Their use has all but eliminated the fall of horses in today's show jumping at that level.

JUMP CUPS

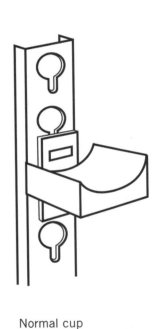

Normal cup

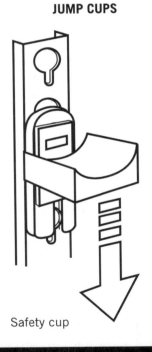

Safety cup

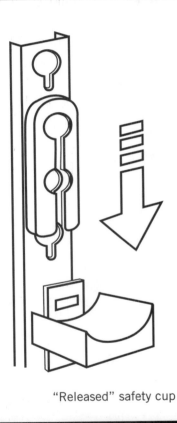

"Released" safety cup

KEY TO THE DIAGRAMS

Here are the symbols you will find on the diagrams and in the keys throughout this book.

Walk	....	Pylon (turning marker)	O	
Trot	– – – –	One canter stride	⊃ ⊃ ⊃ ⊃	
Canter	—— – – —— –	Focal point	👁	
Halt	✕	Ground/Trot-pole	▬▬▬	
Lead change	⊗			

Elevated ground pole or cavalletti	▭▬▭
Cross bar	⋈
Vertical	⊢▭⊣
Oxer	⊨▭▭⊨

Introduction to Exercises

The exercises are divided into Ground Poles, Trot Gymnastics, Canter Exercises, Challenges, and Advanced Exercises. Designed to improve your position and effectiveness as a rider, the series will lead your horse through a sensible training progression — whether he is beginning his career or is already an experienced campaigner.

The first group of exercises, using only simple ground poles, is valuable for both horse and rider even when one of them is at the earliest stage of training. Effectively supplementing your horse's training on the flat, these exercises will ensure that everything your horse has learned in a non-jumping environment will remain uncompromised when jumping enters the equation. They also make a lesson or training session interesting and provide an ongoing "status report" of your progress.

The trot gymnastics are the best way to introduce a horse or rider to jumping. They are equally valuable for continuing to refine the technique of experienced horses, riders, and horse/rider combinations.

Simple canter exercises lead to more complex jumping from the canter. The entire canter series provides an excellent framework for practicing the questions that will be asked on courses in competition. Only the most experienced horses and riders should move directly to the more demanding exercises. Be sure your basic skills are in place!

The final Challenge section specifically addresses various training issues that you may face. The last five exercises ask advanced questions of even the most experienced horse and rider.

Various "Guest Exercises" contributed by world-famous riders and trainers are also included throughout the book.

World champion Rodrigo Pessoa working with Grand Prix winner Joie Gatlin over basic trot-poles.

David O'Connor schooling on the flat.

BASIC EXERCISES FROM THE WALK AND TROT

The following basic exercises cement the absolutely vital elements of straightness, calmness, balance, and rhythm. They improve the jumping performance of every horse and rider. Here you work to establish your confidence and stability along with your horse's cooperation and obedience, all the while avoiding the boredom that results from just "following the arena fence."

> *Straightness, calmness, balance, rhythm*

The entire array of exercises in this first section can be beneficial for everyone, from the greenest horse or most timid rider to the most experienced athlete. If you think jumping looks like fun, yet worry it might be too much for you or your horse, working through these "non-jumping" exercises can help you gain the confidence to go on to the simple gymnastics that follow. One step at a time takes you far in this sport!

Even the most experienced riders and horses can be fooled by the apparent simplicity of these exercises. The question is, can you do them *correctly*? There is good reason Olympic champions spend hours every week incorporating this work into their ongoing training and fitness training programs.

In the beginning, focus on your upper body and leg position while you learn to "feel" your horse's stride length and impulsion. As your horse learns to expect consistent and very specific communication from you, he develops that all-important relaxed, obedient, and cooperative attitude toward his job.

The exercises are presented from simplest to most complicated; we recommend you give them all a try. You may be surprised at which ones are easy or difficult for you or your horse. Ground pole exercises also make a good warm-up for jumping or a fun addition to your normal arena riding.

A real advantage of these early exercises is that you can spend almost limitless amounts of time working on them without imposing the physical toll on your horse that would result from that much actual jumping.

Throughout this book, you will find reminders that should become so ingrained in your riding that they come absolutely naturally!

> *One correct step at a time*
> *is the best way to achieve your goals!*

SETUP

Place two parallel poles, approximately 6 ft., 6 in. to 10 ft. (2 to 3m) apart, in the center of your arena.

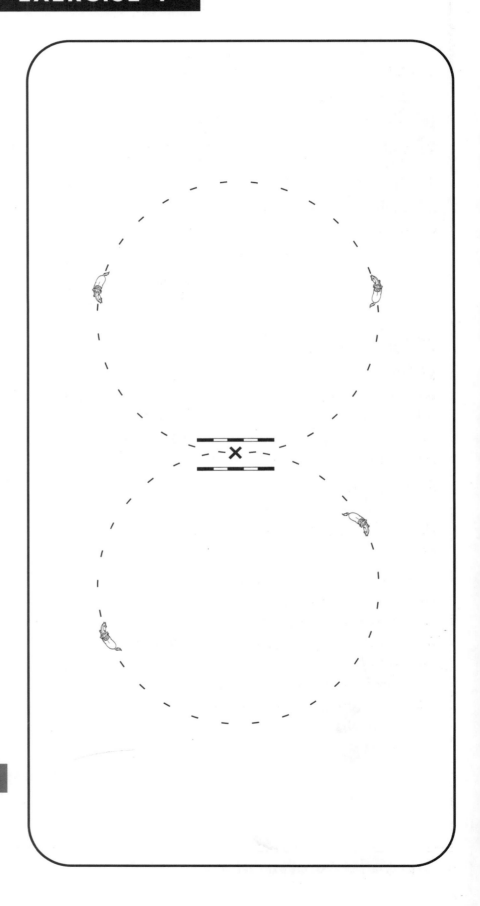

Key

Ground pole ▬▬▬

Trot — — — — —

Halt ✗

A Chute of Poles

How do I ride this?

1. Walk a Figure 8 pattern, using the parallel poles as the center of the 8.

2. Add a halt in the middle of the chute.

3. Trot the Figure 8.

4. Add an occasional halt in the middle of the chute.

5. Vary the pattern by changing direction and alternating between the walk and the trot on different parts of the pattern.

Doublecheck

▶ Are both my circles exactly the same size and truly round?

Try for circles about 33 ft. (10m) in diameter, starting larger at first if need be. The important goal is round and even circles.

▶ Am I using my eyes?

Use your eyes to create (visualize or "see") the track (the path of the circles) before you as you ride.

▶ Is my horse straight when going through the "chute" of the two poles?

A chute of poles artificially controls a horse's side-to-side straightness. In this exercise, you learn to feel what is straight and to use your hands and legs to act as a "chute" when not riding between poles.

▶ Does my horse **bend** properly, following the curve of each circle from nose to tail?

▶ Is my halt **square**?

▶ Is my horse remaining calm and relaxed during the halt as well as throughout the exercise?

▶ Can I move off immediately and smoothly, remaining straight, even in a **transition** from halt to trot?

▶ Am I posting on the correct **diagonal**, changing my diagonal between the poles, without dropping my head to look? Can I *feel* the diagonal?

Benefits

This exercise helps you learn to visualize and execute an accurate track, while establishing a feel for round circles with correct and even bend.

It also helps your horse learn to listen, and to remain calm and under control as you alternate between straightness and bending.

SETUP

Place a single ground pole in the center of your arena.

If the center of your pole does not have a painted stripe, mark it with a piece of tape (electrical or colored plastic tape) to indicate exactly where you want your horse to cross over it.

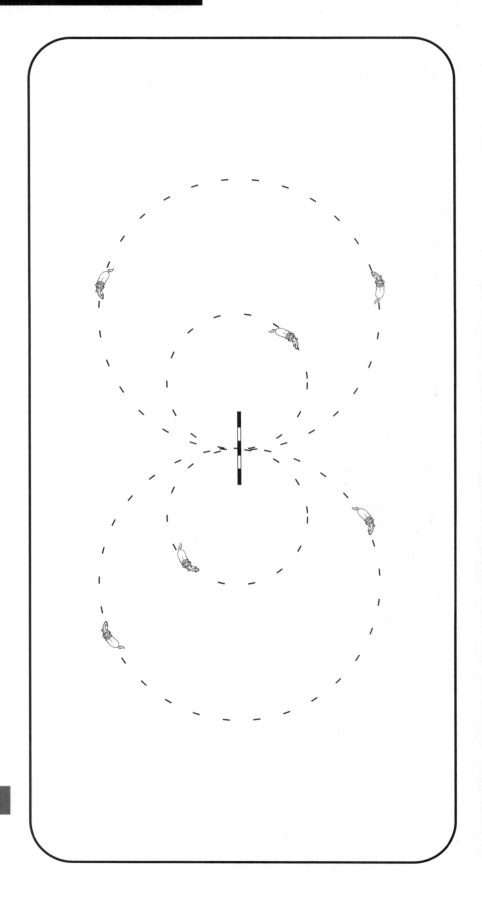

Key

Ground pole ▬▭▬

Trot — — — — — —

THE ROUND FIGURE 8 OVER A SINGLE GROUND POLE

How do I ride this?

1. Walk and trot over the pole, in the Figure 8 pattern shown.

2. Be sure to practice the pattern in both directions and using both a larger and smaller figure 8.

Hints

▶ Make your circles a comfortable size that allows you to maintain an even **pace.**

▶ Always bring your horse to the exact center of the pole (which you have marked).

▶ Whether walking or trotting, establish a relaxed and regular **rhythm** well before the pole, and maintain it over the pole.

WHERE SHOULD I BE LOOKING?

One hears debate over just where a rider should focus when jumping. It is essential to focus first on the center of the obstacle to establish your correct line of approach. Then, as you approach the obstacle on the **track** you have successfully established, it is equally important that you adjust your focus ahead to where you are going next. Your horse will be aware of any abrupt change in where you are looking, especially right in front of an obstacle. It takes conscious practice until it becomes automatic for you to keep your focus the appropriate distance ahead of you at all times.

▶ Strive for very light contact with your horse's mouth. Remember this for all these exercises!

▶ **Focus** on an eye-level point at the end of the arena as your horse travels over the pole. Studying the pole is part of your horse's job, not yours.

Correct. Rider looking ahead to next pole while horse concentrates on the one he is going over.

Incorrect. Rider looking down at ground pole.

SETUP

Set a single ground pole in the center of your arena, where it can be approached at the trot from both directions.

Correct. Two-point position over trot-pole.

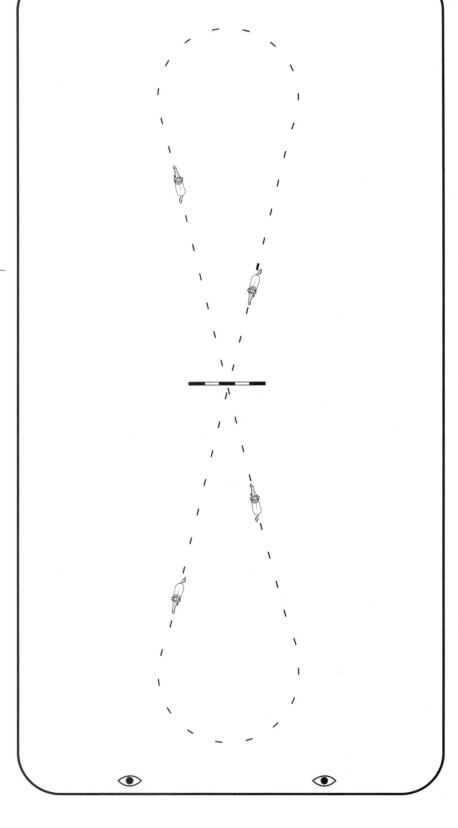

Key

Trot-pole ▰▱▰▱

Trot — — — — —

Focal point 👁

THE LONG FIGURE 8 OVER A SINGLE TROT-POLE

How do I ride this?

1. First walk, then trot, in long, straight lines both approaching and departing from the pole.

2. Connect these lines with symmetrical half circles at each end exactly as shown. You are forming a second, and very different, variety of Figure 8 from that described in Exercise 2.

Make sure your straight lines are truly straight (use a specific **focal point**) and that your half-circles are evenly shaped arcs.

Notice that your horse is crossing the pole at a slight angle each time, rather than on the totally perpendicular approach of the previous exercise.

Doublecheck

▶ Is my horse still maintaining his regular rhythm toward, over, and after the pole, as well as around the half-circles on the ends of the arena?

▶ Does my horse look at the pole and adjust the length of his stride as necessary, without my help and without speeding up or slowing down?

▶ Am I establishing and maintaining my focal point?

▶ Can I avoid tipping forward or falling back as my horse steps over the pole — even when he takes a very short or very long step?

This is the best test of your leg and balance. Be sure you are aware of even the smallest lapse.

Benefits

This exercise combines the concepts of straightness and bend, both necessary practice for any jumping course. When crossing the pole in the middle, you are also introducing your horse to the idea of approaching at an angle. This combination of bending (the turn), then straightening to cross the pole at an angle, is critical for fast and clean jump-offs.

Incorrect. Rider tipping forward, ahead of horse's balance, as horse takes a short step.

Incorrect. Rider falling back as horse takes a longer step over ground pole.

KEY POINT

How Do I Ride in Two-Point?

Two-point position keeps you close to, but not sitting in, the saddle, even to post. Use it to find your correct balance and develop the low center of gravity that is the mark of every effective rider over fences. Your entire weight sinks through the ball of your foot on the stirrup and down into a lowered heel. Maintaining flexibility in all the riding joints (the hips, the knees, the ankles, and the heels) is critical, as bracing or stiffening prevents achieving the balance and security that this position develops.

Pay careful attention to how you get into and out of two-point position. Follow this sequence:

1. While riding at the posting trot, quietly release your whole arm forward and place your hands on your horse's crest approximately one-third of the way between withers and ears, pressing down slightly.

2. Be sure your leg is directly under you and your joints are relaxed — not stiff or braced. Sink your weight into your heel, and cease posting as you find your balance out of the saddle. Don't "stand up," but keep your seat just clear of the saddle. Be sure to keep your head and focus up.

3. Feel all your joints flex softly with your horse's movement as you consciously relax your flat back and maintain a steady and secure position. As your position becomes secure, you will no longer need to rely on your hands to balance your upper body; they can become light and independent.

4. To return to the posting trot, reverse the sequence; pick up your posting rhythm, distributing a part of your weight into your seat again.

5. It is essential to keep your leg in position as you go from two-point to posting. This prevents you from falling back into the saddle.

6. To complete the return to posting trot, bring your elbows back and your hands into normal contact.

7. Practice, practice, practice going into and out of two-point.

Your skill and ease in moving among a light seat, a full seat, and two-point position determine your security over jumps and your ability to assist your horse in whatever manner the job at hand requires.

THE SINGLE TROT-POLE IN TWO-POINT POSITION

Setup

Set a single trot-pole in the center of your arena where it can be approached from both directions (the same as in the previous exercise).

How do I ride this?

1. Trot the pattern shown in Exercise 3, maintaining a two-point position throughout the length of the straight lines.

2. Resume a posting trot around the half circles at each end of the arena.

Hints

The balance of your upper body is largely determined by the position and security of your lower leg. Be aware of even the smallest shift in your balance.

▶ If your balance tips too far ahead so you fall on your hands when your horse takes a shortened step over the pole, then your lower leg is weak and slipping back too easily or too far.

▶ If your seat falls back into the saddle when your horse takes an extended step over the pole, your seat is too heavy and your lower leg is too far forward or your knee is rigid.

Benefits

It is well worth spending the time necessary to improve your position. The pay-off comes when you are jumping.

Developing a strong and secure position is essential for both you and your horse to reach the highest levels you can achieve.

Correct. Two-point position over trot-pole.

> *Developing a strong and secure position is essential for both you and your horse to reach the highest levels you can achieve.*

SETUP

Place two trot-poles in a straight line, approximately 50 ft. (15m) apart, so that you can approach them from either direction.

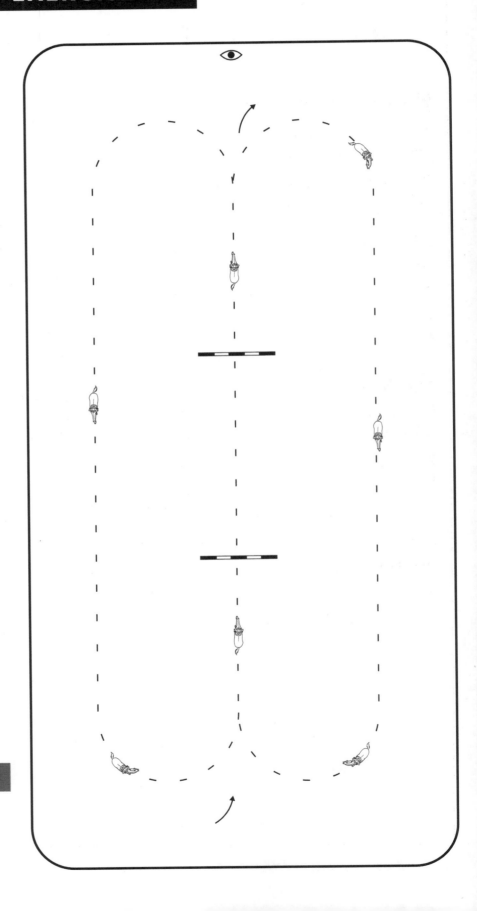

Key

Trot-pole	▬▭▬
Trot	– – – – –
Focal point	◉

TWO TROT-POLES

How do I ride this?

1. Ride a straight line over the center of both poles at the posting trot.

2. If your horse does not meet the second pole "on stride" while maintaining consistent rhythm and strides, have your helper roll one pole to make the distance a bit shorter or longer.

3. Trot the two poles in both directions. Plan in advance the track you will follow to change direction.

Doublecheck

▶ Am I crossing the poles exactly in the middle every time?

▶ Is my horse's pace consistent before, between, and after the poles?

▶ Is my balance steady? Is my horse's?

▶ Can I correct my balance easily when necessary?

▶ Am I anticipating the pole and/or getting ahead of my horse?

Reminder

Be especially vigilant for any tendency to **anticipate** or **get ahead**. This often results from worrying about being **left behind**. The solution is to correct your leg and basic position so that you can smoothly *follow* your horse's movements and no longer feel the need to second-guess what he might do next.

Variation

Alternate between posting and two-point position over the poles, switching from posting over the first pole to two-point for the second, and vice versa. Your horse should not change pace when you change your position.

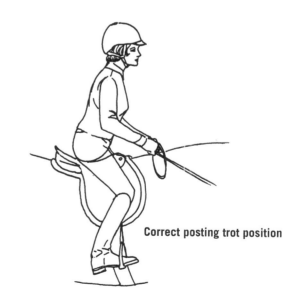

Correct posting trot position

EXERCISE 6

SETUP

Place two parallel poles in a straight line, with approximately 13 to14 ft. (4 to 4.3m) between them. These poles are A and D on the diagram. Have your helper ready to add two more poles at B and C.

Incorrect. Horse jumping over trot-poles.

Correct. Relaxed trot over trot-poles.

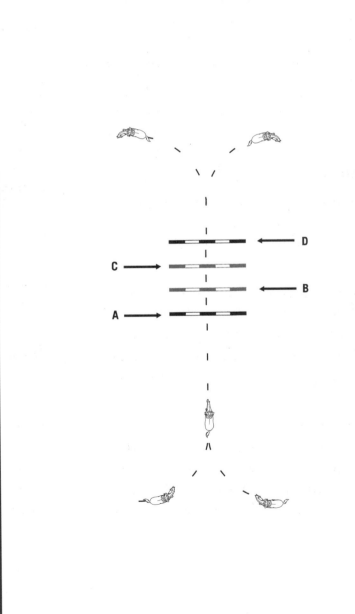

Key

Trot-pole ▬▬▬

Trot – – – – – –

A GRID OF TROT-POLES
Determining Your Horse's Natural Stride Length at the Medium Trot

How do I ride this?

1. Ride your horse at a relaxed, medium trot in a straight line back and forth over both poles.

2. Observe if your horse negotiates both poles easily without changing his pace. Leading with either front leg, he should take one step over the first pole, take two more strides between the poles, and step over the second pole with the opposite leg.

3. If the distance you begin with does not fit your horse's stride, have your helper adjust the distance between the poles so that your horse can maintain even strides over and between the poles.

4. Repeat this exercise until your horse is very relaxed and willingly maintains an even pace — neither speeding up or slowing down.

5. Without moving pole A or D, have your helper add the two additional poles, first pole B and then C, as you continue to trot through the exercise. If necessary, make any final adjustment to fit your horse's medium trot.

6. Have your helper measure and make a note of the spacing between the poles. This is the distance we will consider *your* horse's natural stride length at the quiet, medium trot you will be using for many of these exercises.

Doublecheck

▶ Can I feel which of my horse's leg steps over the pole first?

▶ Am I focusing up, content to let my horse concentrate on the poles?

▶ Can I feel an increasing regularity and deliberation in my horse's trot as he becomes proficient at this exercise?

TROT GRID SPACING

For most horses, a trot stride is approximately 4 ft., 6 in. (1.4m). It can vary, however, especially for ponies or horses with exceptionally short or long strides.

In any exercises that call for a trot grid, set your trot-poles at this distance. As you proceed with the work, you can shorten or lengthen this basic distance to help your horse develop a greater natural range in stride — from short to long.

Reminders

It is very important that the horse is relaxed and attentive over two, three, and four poles at the trot before progressing to the next exercises.

To deal with a horse that has become apprehensive, go back to Exercise 5. Trot to the first pole, then come down to a walk on a loose rein to go over the second.

Changing a nervous or tense attitude calls for lots of repetition and a calm and patient rider.

SETUP

Place parallel poles as in Exercise 6, but raise alternating ends of each pole onto blocks.

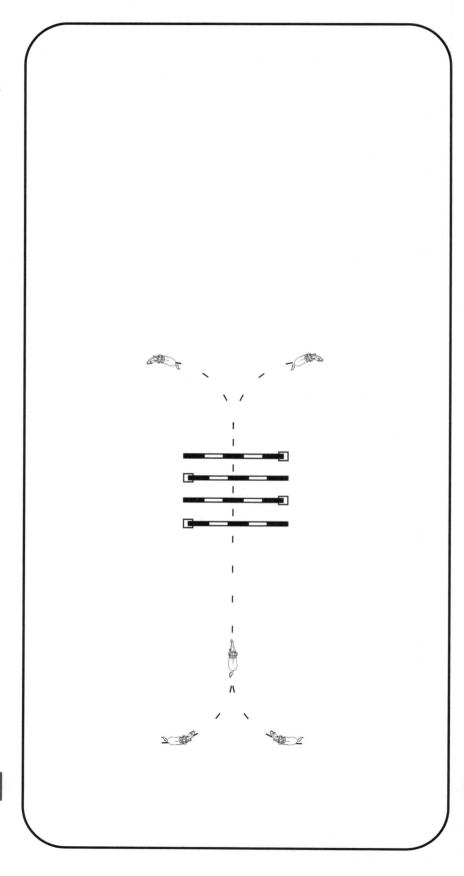

THE PARTIALLY ELEVATED TROT GRID

How do I ride this?

1. Ride straight through the middle of the poles, maintaining an even pace at the posting trot. Post with a definite rhythm to help your horse establish and maintain his own balance.

2. Your horse should remain calm, yet attentive. He must be given the opportunity to learn how to retain (or regain) his balance and rhythm, even on those occasions when he meets the first pole a bit "off-stride," that is, in a way that requires him to make a real adjustment to his stride to step over it cleanly.

Problem solving

▶ I get left behind (even a little bit) when my horse takes the springier steps necessary over these elevated poles.

Try relaxing your back and lightening your seat, or, if necessary, maintain a two-point position through the poles a few times.

▶ My horse "stubs his toes" — touching or tripping over the poles.

Let him learn by making his own mistakes. Bumping a pole provides the motivation for him to learn.

▶ My horse tries to jump one or more of the poles.

*Return to the simpler version of the exercise and repeat it in a relaxed manner until your horse becomes calm again. **Never** punish or resort to rough hands.*

Benefits

Raising alternate ends of the poles before elevating both ends (coming next, in Exercise 8) defines the straight line you need to ride through the grid. This allows you to concentrate and establish your calmness, balance, and rhythm before moving on to the next exercise.

Trot-pole elevated on one end.

EXERCISE 8

SETUP

Start with two trot-poles set at your horse's optimal trot stride distance (see Exercise 6). Add a third pole at the same spacing, then a fourth and fifth. Make sure your horse continues to maintain one stride over each pole. Next, raise the alternate ends of each pole onto blocks. Finally, elevate both ends of your poles onto the blocks.

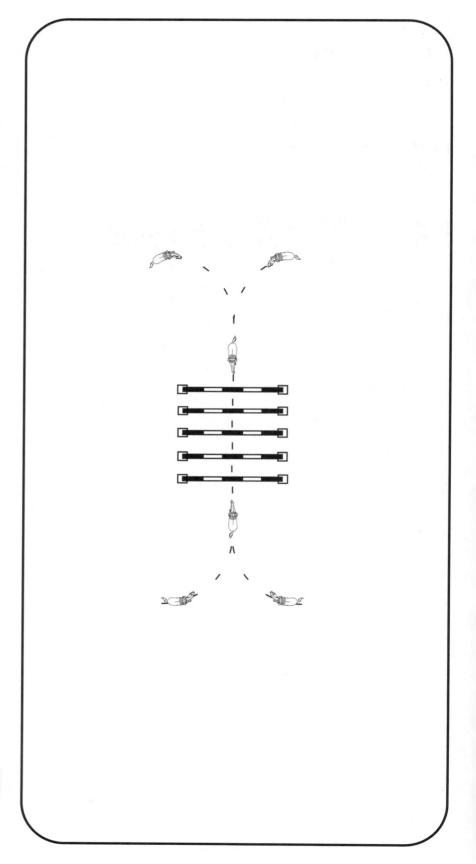

BUILDING A RAISED GRID OF TROT-POLES

How do I ride this?

Your job is to ride through the middle of the grid and maintain the same regular trot as the grid expands from two easy poles into the more difficult, longer grid of raised poles.

POSITION CHECK

As you ride your horse over the raised grids at the trot, the security and flexibility of your position will be tested. If your seat is too heavy in the saddle, you will be "caught behind the motion" by the second or third pole. If you get "ahead" of your horse at the first pole, you will be making the exercise difficult for both of you.

A properly positioned lower leg, along with a relaxed and light seat in impeccable balance, will reward you with a remarkable feeling of rhythm and power.

Benefits

A longer, raised trot grid will help your horse, when he is ready for this challenge, to develop greater engagement, strength, balance, regularity of stride, and attentiveness. For this reason, this exercise can be a valuable addition to a training regime for horses going on to upper-level dressage work, as well as jumping.

Am I ready for the next step?

You have to gauge when your horse has gained the required skills and fitness to succeed over a longer grid when both ends of each pole are raised. The higher the poles are set, the more energy and concentration required on the part of your horse. Even a moderate 2 to 4 in. (5 to 10cm) elevation causes your horse to work harder; only a strong, fit, and experienced horse can be expected to trot a line of poles raised to a more challenging 10 to 12 in. (25 to 30cm) height.

SETUP

Lay out a straight line of approximately six poles down the center of your arena. Set a distance of 9 ft. (2.8m) — or double your horse's ideal trot stride distance — between them (see Exercise 6).

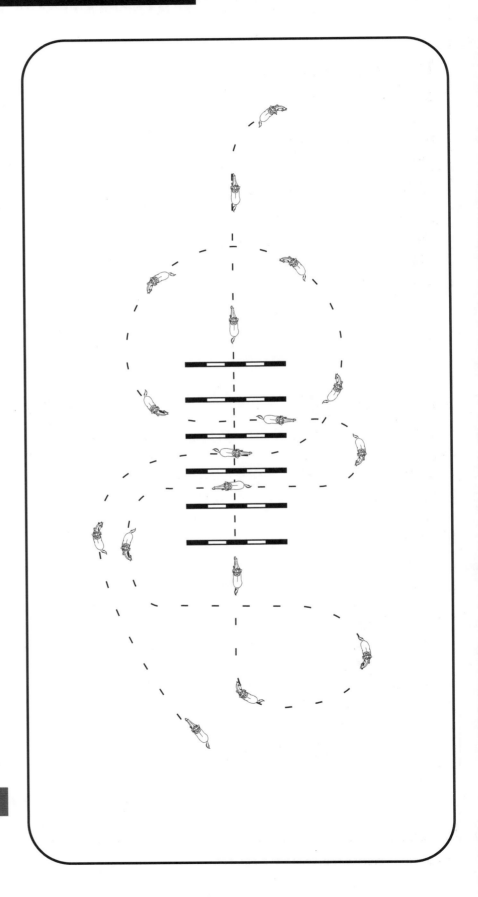

SERPENTINES THROUGH POLES

How do I ride this?

1. Ride between the rails at a trot, creating the even serpentine tracks shown. Go between every third pole to make larger loops until you are comfortable.

2. Next, try every other pole.

3. Finish by trotting up over the poles. (Note that this spacing allows your horse to complete one full stride in between each of the poles.)

4. Repeat the exercise in both directions.

5. Try planning and executing a pattern with varying loops.

Problem solving

▶ I'm getting lost and going between the wrong poles.

Visualize, reviewing the complete course in your mind before you begin. When you execute the exercise, remember to continually move your focus ahead.

Benefits

Here you practice planning and visualization — the first steps to memorizing long jumping courses.

Your horse will look to you for clear direction as to where he is to go: when to bend or turn, and when to travel straight.

As you practice, you will find a flow to your track that will make it easy to maintain symmetrical loops on your attentive and relaxed horse.

Am I ready for the next step?

▶ Do you feel comfortable in planning and riding a variety of fairly intricate patterns at the posting trot both through and over the poles?

▶ Is your horse obediently responding to your guidance, retaining his even pace throughout?

EXERCISE 10

SETUP

Place two sets of three trot-poles, set to the distance of your horse's medium stride (see Exercise 6), in the middle of your arena. Leave approximately 20 to 30 ft. (6 to 9m) between the trot-pole sets.

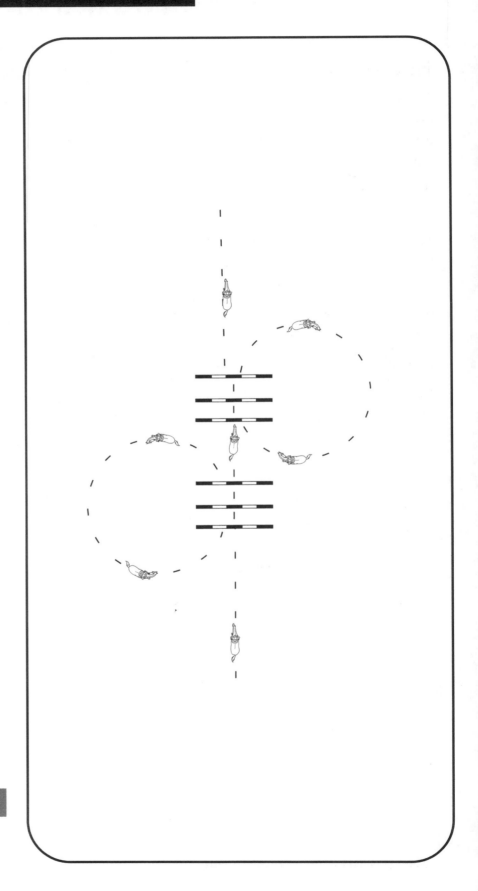

Key

Trot-pole ▬▬▬▬

Trot – – – – –

SHORT TROT GRIDS WITH CIRCLES

How do I ride this?

1. Trot straight through the first set of poles, then turn immediately and make a medium circle to either the left or the right.

2. Proceed once again over the first set of poles, completing your circle.

3. Continue straight toward and through the second set of poles.

4. Ride a second circle, in the opposite direction from the first, to bring you back through the second set again.

5. Repeat in the opposite direction.

6. Reverse direction for the first and second circles.

Problem solving

▶ My circles aren't round or equal in size.
Visualize, concentrate, and feel the bend in your horse's body.

▶ My horse changes speed or raises his head when going from straight line to circle or vice versa.
Smooth and soften your aids — especially your hands — while you retain an even posting rhythm throughout the exercise.

Benefits

Alternating bending and straightening, including strides over poles, helps your horse to soften and listen to your aids. He will learn to maintain his regular rhythm along with a soft, light, and consistent contact with your hands.

SETUP

Set four poles approximately 35 ft. (10.7m) apart.

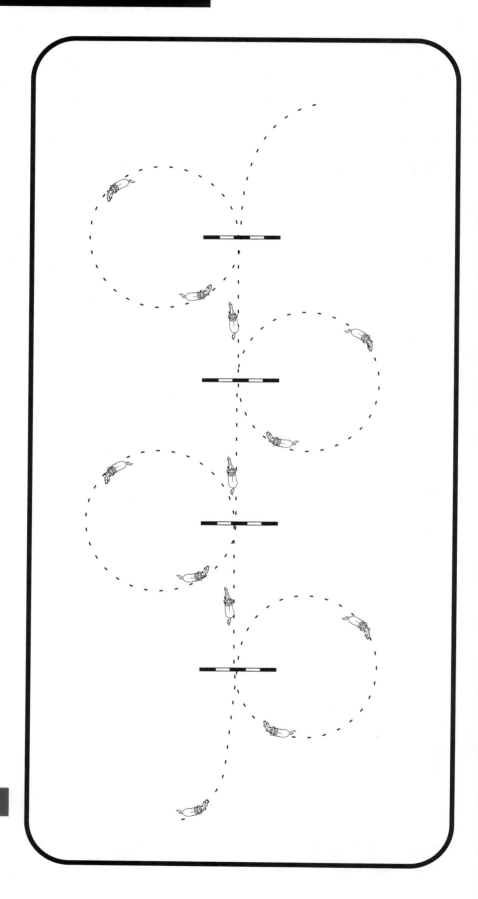

Key

Trot-pole ▬▭▬▭▬

Medium trot - - - - - - - - -

POLES AND CIRCLES

How do I ride this?

1. Trot over the center of the first pole, then make a 33 ft. (10m) circle that takes you back over that pole a second time.

2. Proceed over the second pole, followed by another 10 meter circle in the opposite direction.

3. Continue through all four poles in this manner, alternating the direction of your circles.

Doublecheck

▶ Can I feel the correct bend — the shape of my horse's body — as I ride this exercise?

▶ Is my circle truly round and even (no corners allowed)?

*Learn to feel **cutting in** or **bulging**. Then, take measures to prevent these tendencies, through proper use of your aids (legs, seat, and hands). Teaching your horse to execute correct circles now makes all your future training so much easier.*

WHAT'S SO SPECIAL ABOUT CIRCLES?

Correct circles are surprisingly difficult. Making truly round ones, in a precise size and location, takes practice and is more often part of the basic training for dressage riders than for hunter or jumper riders. Controlling your focus (eyes) and learning to feel the proper bend in your horse are essential. Given the opportunity, most horses want to **cut in** (flatten) on one side of a circle while bulging out on the other side.

Each and every turn on a jumper course is a part of a circle. Making smooth and accurate turns is essential to riding well over jumps.

Practice until this skill becomes a natural part of your riding. You'll be amazed at how much you can improve your results.

SETUP

Place two poles parallel to each other approximately 9 ft. (2.75m) apart.

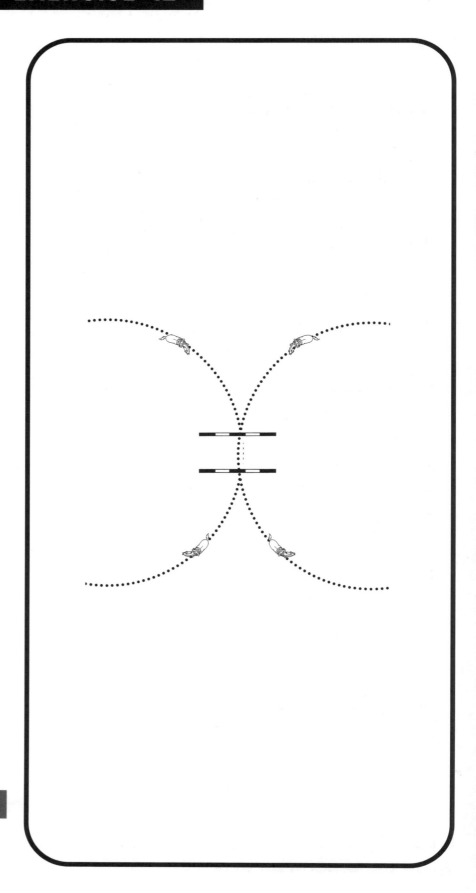

COUNTING STEPS

A Guest Exercise with Joe Fargis, Show Jumping Olympic Individual and Team Gold Medal winner, 1984, and Team Silver Medal winner, 1988

How do I ride this?

1. While walking your horse over the poles in a relaxed manner, see if you can correctly count the number of strides your horse takes between them.

2. Have your helper change the distance without you knowing whether the poles were moved closer together or placed farther apart.

3. Continue to feel and count the number of strides at various distances.

Doublecheck

▶ Is my horse stepping over the poles in an even, rhythmic manner?

▶ Can I consistently feel how many strides my horse is fitting between the poles?

▶ Are we maintaining a calm, relaxed attitude?

▶ Can I feel where my horse's feet are without looking down?

Next step

When you are ready, see if you can influence your horse to take longer strides so that the same number of steps covers a longer distance; then try shortening your horse's walk to fit an extra step between the poles.

▶ Can you ask for a lengthening of your horse's stride (**extension**) without quickening?

▶ Can you ask for a shortening of stride (**collection**) with quiet hands and without inhibiting your horse's rhythm?

Benefits

This builds your awareness of smoothness, calmness, straightness, and accuracy, elements that are absolutely critical to jumping.

> "Horses are living, breathing creatures. Treat them as you wish to be treated — with kindness — and they will give back to you."
>
> — Joe Fargis,
> 1984 Olympic double Gold Medal winner

SETUP

Place two poles on the side of the arena about 50 ft. (15m) apart. Add two more as shown in the diagram to use when changing direction.

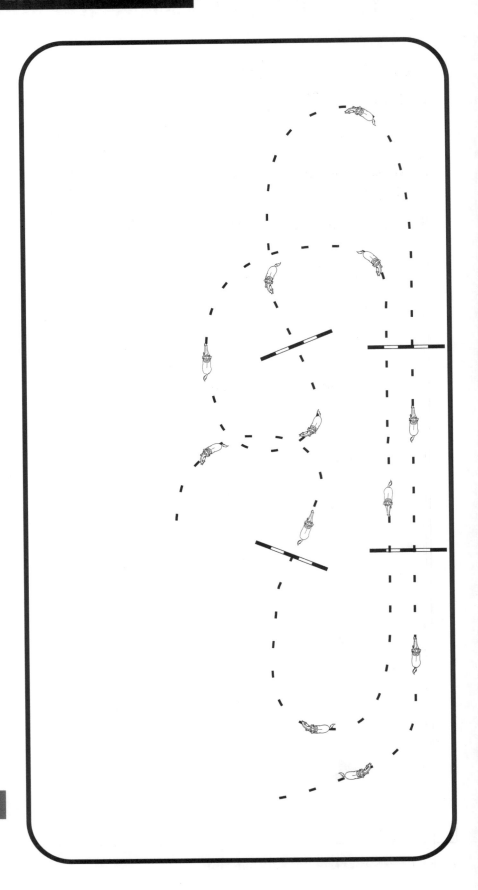

Key

Trot-pole ▬▭▬

Trot - - - - - - - - - - - - -

Trot-Poles Using Different Stride Lengths

How do I ride this?

1. Start with a **medium trot** over the center of both poles. Concentrate on keeping the strides uniform in length.

2. Make a loop around and over one of the single poles.

3. Finish by going back over the two poles in the opposite direction.

4. When your horse is relaxed and consistent, count the number of strides your horse takes between the poles at his medium trot.

5. Ride toward the two poles at the trot again, this time using a **shortened stride**. Be sure to maintain an even rhythm in your shortened trot.

6. Count the steps and see how many more you are now taking.

7. Return to your medium trot over the poles.

8. Trot them with a **lengthened stride**, maintaining your rhythm.

9. Count the steps. How many steps have you dropped?

Doublecheck

▶ Can I plan ahead and achieve one, two, or even three steps fewer or more by adjusting my horse's stride length?

▶ Can I adjust my horse's stride without his becoming lethargic or **quick?**

▶ Can I feel the rhythm and achieve a longer stride (longer posting interval) rather than a faster gait (quicker posting rhythm)?

▶ Can I always return to the medium trot without interrupting my rhythm?

▶ Is my position solid, or do I lose my balance more easily when trotting the poles at a lengthened trot?

Benefits

This exercise involves setting the rhythm and desired stride length well in advance of an obstacle and maintaining it between obstacles. This skill is especially important for success in the hunter division.

It is important that the length of stride and even rhythm be well established before the first obstacle and maintained until well after the second one.

SETUP

Set two poles on the side of the arena about 50 ft. (15m) apart. Set two additional poles as shown in the diagram (the same as in Exercise 13). As in Exercise 13, the two additional poles are used for changing direction.

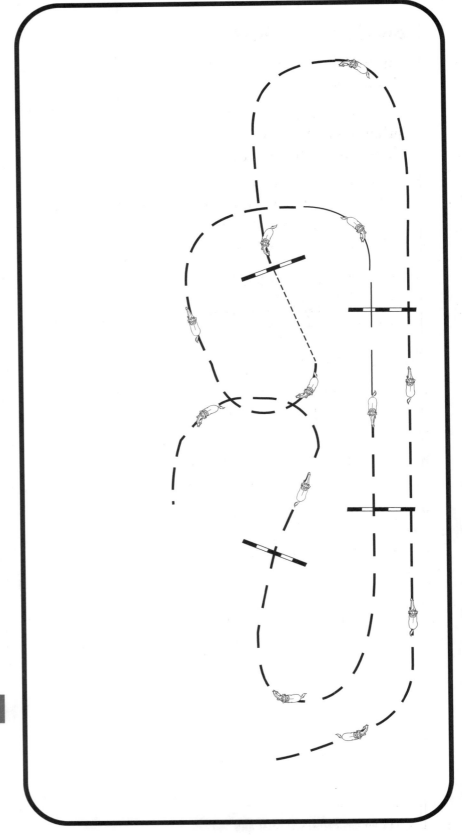

Key

Trot-pole ▬▭▬▭▬

Medium trot — — — — — —

Lengthened trot —— — — —— —

Shortened trot -------------------

TRANSITIONS IN PACE OVER TWO POLES

How do I ride this?

1. Approach and execute the first rail at a medium trot.

2. Immediately after the first pole, lengthen your trot and maintain the longer stride toward and over the second pole.

3. Next, try a lengthened trot toward and over the first pole, shortening your trot immediately and maintaining the shortened trot over the second one.

> With horses, repetition works well; temper not at all.

Doublecheck

▶ Are my transitions smooth; am I preparing my horse for what comes next using subtle aids?

▶ Am I remembering to extend my horse's stride rather than allowing him to quicken?

▶ Is my horse achieving a truly short stride when asked, without resisting my hands and without walking or stopping by mistake?

Problem solving

▶ Instead of a trot on a lengthened stride, my horse breaks into the canter in front of or over a rail.

Make sure you are not being abrupt with your aids or throwing your upper body forward when you ask him to lengthen. Concentrate on smooth and gradual transitions.

Benefits

Immediate and imperceptible transitions are the keys to a smooth (and, if in a jump-off, fast) jumping round.

CORRECTING MISTAKES

A good general rule is:

1. Always correct your mistake as quickly and quietly as possible as you continue to complete the exercise.

2. Then, before repeating the exercise, figure out how you can prevent the same mistake occurring the next time.

EXERCISE 15

SETUP

Set three poles along the side of the arena, approximately 60 to 70 ft. (18 to 21m) apart. Add two additional poles as shown to use while reversing direction.

KEEPING YOUR MIND IN FRONT OF YOUR HORSE

This concept is key to riding jumping courses. It means that you must anticipate and plan your *next* move or step *while* you correctly ride the current step. For example, when your horse is in the air over a jump, you are already preparing for the next jump or turn with your eyes, your hands, your legs, and your body. Your brain must be several steps ahead of your horse!

Key

Trot-pole

Medium trot

Shortened trot

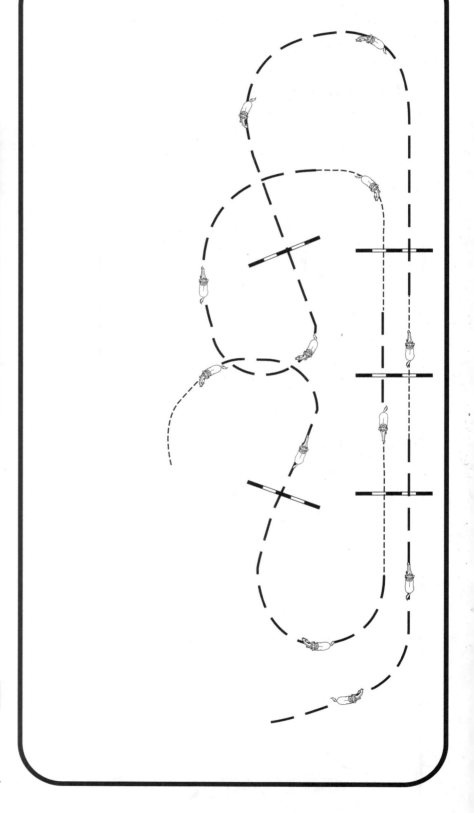

ADDING A THIRD POLE (AND ANOTHER TRANSITION)

How do I ride this?

1. Using what you have learned in the previous exercise, make two transitions within the line, between each of the poles.

2. Ride the first and third pole at one stride length, and the middle one at another. For example, medium trot to the first pole, shortened trot to the second pole, and medium trot to the third pole. Or, shortened trot to the first pole, medium to the second pole, and shortened again to the third.

3. To make this exercise more challenging, use a lengthened trot in place of medium.

> *Knowing exactly what you want — and how to use the minimum necessary to accomplish it — are important keys to good horsemanship.*

Doublecheck

▶ Can I maintain straightness and even rhythm over all three poles while showing a clear difference between medium, long, and short stride lengths?

Problem solving

We missed the transition or are almost upon the next pole before completing it.

*Focus is key here; have the plan clear in your mind before beginning and **keep your mind in front of your horse** throughout every exercise.*

Your horse resists when asked to shorten his stride.

Your hands are too rough or you've done insufficient basic work in the preceding exercises. Give yourself more distance between the poles so you can be sure to accomplish the shortening you've asked for — without being rough.

Knowing exactly what you want — and how you need to accomplish it — are key to good horsemanship.

Am I ready for the next step?

▶ Are both you and your horse confident and proficient in establishing a pace and performing multiple transitions in stride length over the poles?

▶ Does your horse respond without either resisting your hand when asked to shorten or ignoring your leg when asked to lengthen?

Benefits

This basic exercise is excellent for establishing effective communication between you and your horse. It teaches you to use your aids smoothly and clearly, while your horse becomes accustomed to looking to you for specific and clear instructions.

EXERCISE 16

SETUP

Start with two poles centered on opposite sides of a 66 ft. (20m) diameter circle.

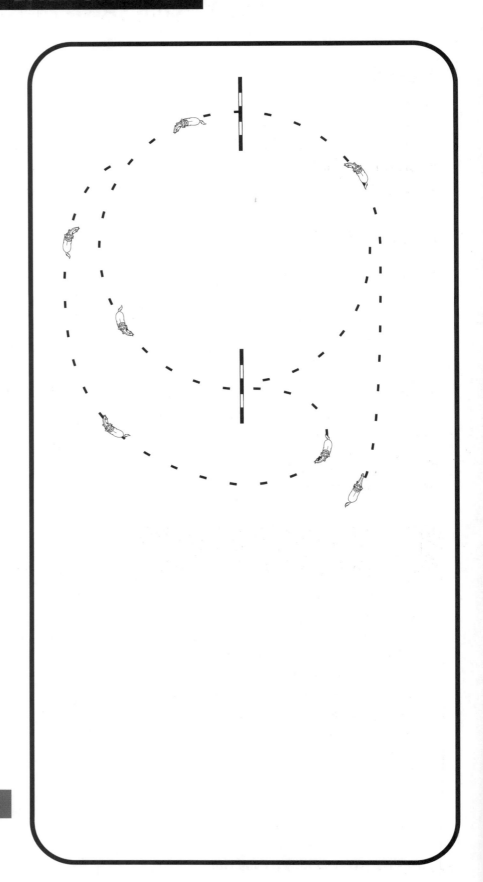

Key

Trot-pole ▬▬▬

Medium trot ▬ ▬ ▬ ▬ ▬

TROT-POLES ON THE CIRCLE

How do I ride this?

1. Ride around the full circle three to five times at the trot, keeping each half of the circle symmetrical. Cross the exact center of both rails each time.

2. Repeat in both directions.

Doublecheck

▶ Are my circles perfectly round?

▶ Where on each circle does my horse tend to turn too easily (cut in); and where on the circle is he more resistant to turning (bulging out)?

▶ Is my horse maintaining a bend in his body that exactly conforms to the shape of the circle, even over the poles?

▶ Am I centered on my horse and following his body around the circle?

Benefits

The ability to ride symmetrical circles and to "place" your horse on a circle or turn *exactly* where you want him to be is critical to accurate riding and jumping.

Accurate corners are essential to successful jumping. This exercise helps you learn to recognize and correct every horse's natural tendency to bulge out and cut in on turns.

Reminder

Horses aren't foaled with a knack for performing precise circles. You must be a smart and effective rider first to note the horse's natural tendencies to cut in or bulge and then use your aids to create that perfectly symmetrical circle.

USING A LUNGE LINE TO SET A CIRCLE

For a 20-meter circle, measure 33 ft. (10 m) on your lunge line. Have your helper hold the line at the 10-meter mark (or use a full water bucket as an anchor if you're on your own). Take the end of the lunge line and walk around the line holder in a circle, making a corresponding line in the sand with your boot. Place the center of two poles perpendicular to the curve.

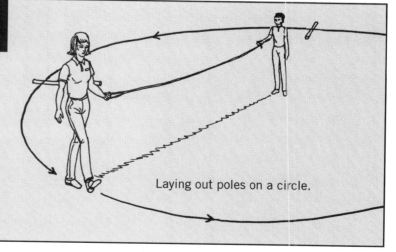

Laying out poles on a circle.

SETUP

Start with two rails centered on opposite sides of a 66 ft. (20m) diameter circle. See "Using a Lunge Line to Set a Circle" in Exercise 16. Add a pole at C. There are now three ground poles on your perfect circle.

First ride the circle over the three poles, then add the final one. You now have poles at all four points on the compass.

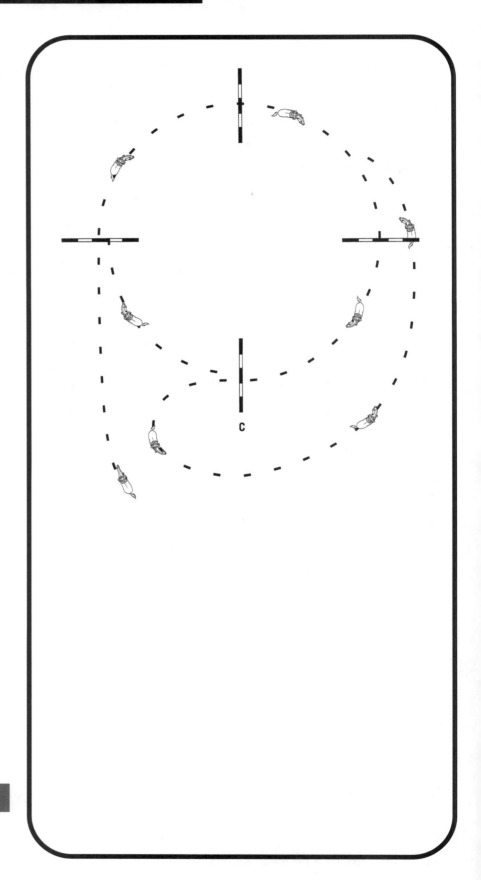

Key

Trot-pole ▬ ▭ ▬ ▭

Medium trot — — — — — —

COMPLETING THE CIRCLE

How do I ride this?

1. Trot the circle, being sure to pass over the center of each pole every time around.

2. Maintaining an even trot rhythm and the same correct bend, aim to achieve the same number of strides in each quadrant of the circle.

3. Work in both directions, with extra time spent in your horse's stiffest direction.

Doublecheck

▶ Am I keeping my eyes up, consistently moving my focus ahead to the next rail, and visually "drawing" the circle to keep it smooth and round, so all four quadrants are identical?

▶ Is my horse taking the same number of strides between each pole?

▶ Am I centered on my horse? Is my horse balanced?

Benefits

Most horses have one direction they find easier to bend or turn toward. A horse that finds one direction difficult and resists the aids is said to be "stiff" in that direction. Work quietly and persistently until your horse is equally comfortable bending to both the left and the right.

Reminders

This exercise is harder than it appears! To do it correctly, in a true circle, requires coordination between inner and outer leg aids, along with effective yet soft hands.

▶ First recognize, and then correct, even the subtlest tilt in your horse's balance.

▶ Stiff and resistant horses don't do this exercise well at first.

▶ Quiet repetition helps.

SETUP

Building from Exercise 17, place three more rails on the other side of your circle to make a second circle. The middle rail is shared by the two circles, creating a Figure 8 pattern.

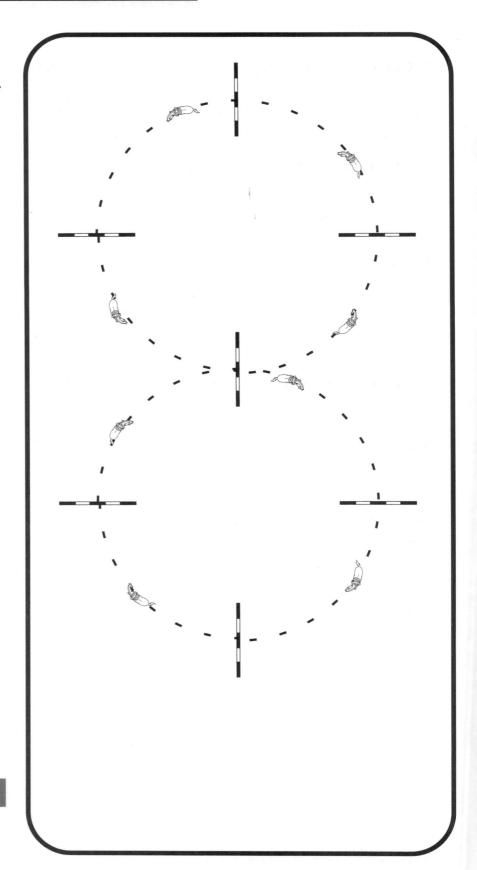

Key

Trot-pole ▬▬▬▬

Medium trot — — — — — —

ADJOINING CIRCLES

How do I ride this?

1. Trot one complete circle, then ride a Figure 8 pattern, changing the bend over the common pole.

2. Repeat this in both directions.

3. For variety, occasionally complete two or three circles before changing direction.

Doublecheck

▶ Am I anticipating the next quadrant of the circle by remembering how my horse felt the previous times around?

▶ Am I planning for and accomplishing a correct change in my horse's bend over the pole common to both circles?

Problem solving

My circles don't match.

Since most horses (like most people) have a stiffer side, you have to work a bit harder to maintain the bend when going in that direction. Ride extra circles in your horse's more difficult direction.

Benefits

The change in direction added here adds variety and some difficulty to this seemingly simple exercise.

Correct. Rider looking ahead to next pole while horse concentrates on the one he is going over.

SETUP

Set four poles in a star pattern with approximately 20 ft. (6m) between the ends of the poles.

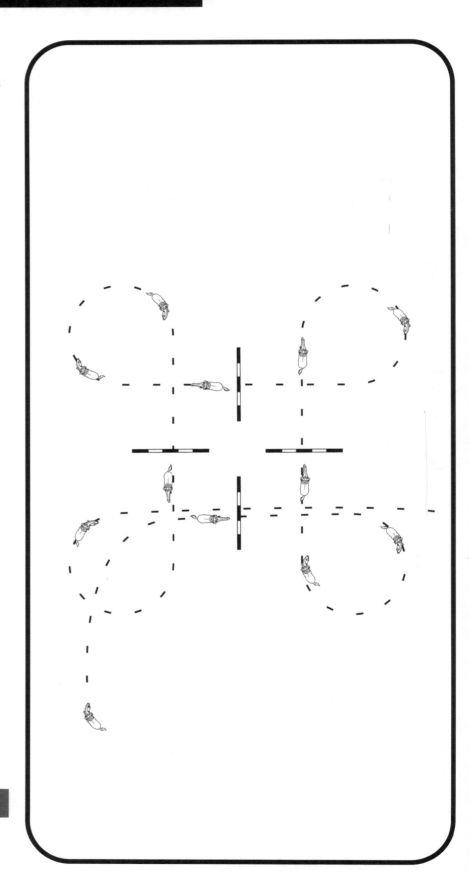

Key

Trot-pole ▬▬▭▬

Medium trot — —   —   —   —   —

FOUR-LEAF CLOVER

How do I ride this?

1. Trot across one pole; make a circle by turning away from the star, until you are facing the second pole.

2. Trot over that pole, following with a circle.

3. Continue until you have trotted over all four rails in this manner.

Doublecheck

▶ Am I planning and completing each circle so that I am lined up directly perpendicular with the center of the next pole each time?

▶ Are all my circles the same size?

> *Good horsemen have the patience to repeat and repeat and know when "enough is enough."*

Benefits

This is an especially good exercise for horses that are stiff in one direction or the other. Use both directions, putting more emphasis on the horse's stiffer side.

The repetition of straightening and repeating a bend in the same direction helps a stiff horse to accept your aids.

REPETITION

Repetition is usually the most effective means of approaching a problem. Make sure the work is done quietly and methodically. Always remember to reward any effort on your horse's part for trying something new or difficult, as well as for a job well done.

Good horsemen have the patience to repeat and repeat and yet are careful to discern when "enough is enough."

SETUP

Repeat the setup from Exercise 19.

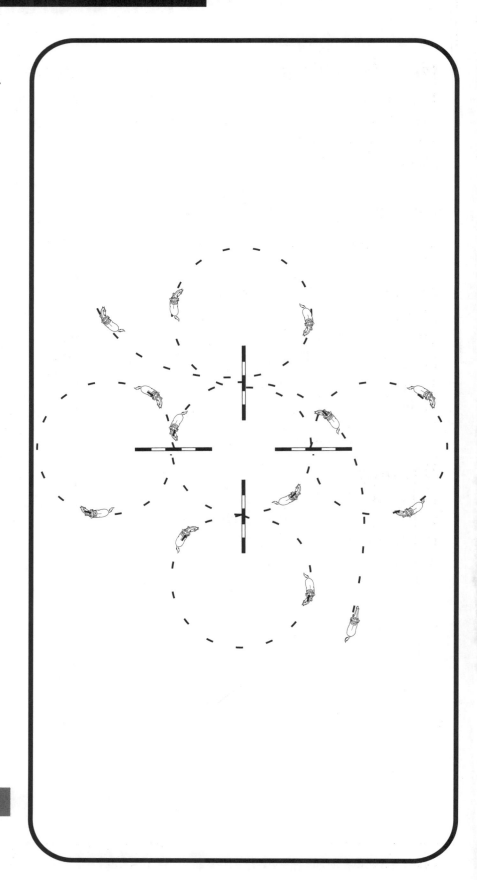

A STAR OF POLES WITH FOUR CIRCLES

How do I ride this?

1. Ride the bending line over two consecutive poles, followed by a circle to the outside. This circle takes you back over the second pole again.

2. Continue on a bend to the next pole, followed by another circle to the outside.

3. Continue this pattern. Finish over the first pole.

4. Ride this pattern in both directions, remembering to trot directly over the middle of the poles.

5. Concentrate on the changes in bend. Bend in one direction between the two poles, followed by a circle on the opposite bend.

Reminder

Riding this correctly, with smooth changes in bend and a steady rhythm, requires flexibility and obedience from your horse, as well as more effective aids from you.

Benefits

▶ The emphasis on bending is valuable for suppling your horse, especially if you repeat the exercise with the poles closer together (down to approximately 10 ft. [3m] between the pole ends).

▶ A horse must have power, flexibility, and obedience to manage the exercise at this level of difficulty, as it requires a lot of collection.

USE GOOD JUDGMENT

This type of exercise can become somewhat stressful, physically and mentally, to your horse. While the exercise is a good test of a horse's level of concentration as well as development of both sides of his "engine" (i.e., hindquarters), it's best to ride this only once or twice in each direction before taking a break.

EXERCISE 21

SETUP

Place four poles in the "**W**" pattern shown in Diagram A. Set the angles so that the distances between the centers of each pole accommodate your horse's trot.

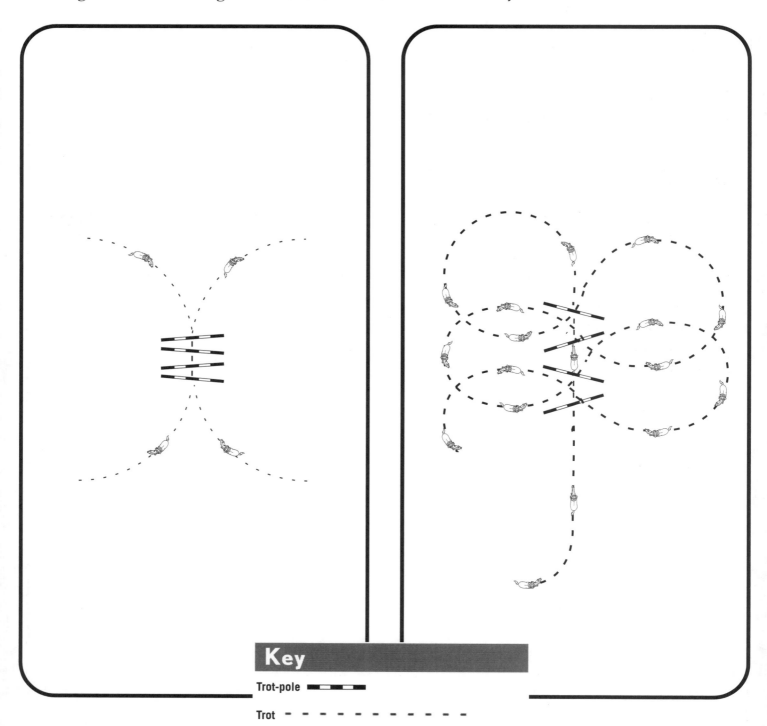

Key

Trot-pole ▬ ▭ ▬

Trot - - - - - - - - -

Medium trot — — — — —

Diagram A

Diagram B (Variation)

"W" (Angled) Trot-Poles

How do I ride this?

1. Trot straight through the center of the poles, as though riding a normal trot grid (see Exercise 8). Your task is to ride absolutely straight; any drifting off center creates the wrong spacing between poles.

2. Use your hand and leg aids to create a straight horse traveling on a straight and precisely located line.

Problem solving

▶ I can't stay straight through the grid.
Are you looking down at the poles in an attempt to steer? Keep your focus ahead — this is the key to straightness.

▶ My horse is tripping and not stepping smoothly between the poles.
Are you riding through the exact center of the line?

Variations

▶ Try increasing the angles as shown in Diagram B. This spacing accommodates one full trot stride between each rail, as well as the steps over each.

▶ Follow a line straight through the poles with a serpentine back over each individual pole in a Figure 8 pattern; finish with a second trip up the center of the poles.

Am I ready for the next step?

If you can keep each loop of the serpentine completely uniform in size and pace with your horse beginning and finishing straight up the grid, you are progressing toward a real working partnership with your horse.

SETUP

Place your trot-poles perpendicular to the arc of a 66 ft. (20m) circle in a fan shape. Center the poles on the track of the circle and set the distance between them for your horse's normal stride. (Refer to Exercise 16 for a hint on an easy way to set this up.)

For horses at a higher level of training, you can ride with the poles set on as small as a 33 ft. (10m) circle.

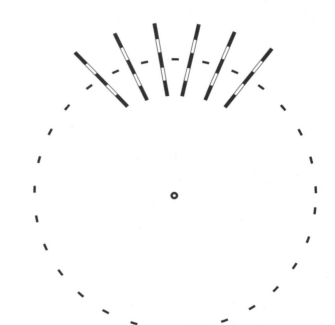

Using a 66 ft. (20m) circle

Using a (more difficult) 33 ft. (10m) circle

Key

Trot-pole ▰▰▰▰▰

Medium trot — — — — — —

Pylon ◉

TROT GRID ON A CIRCLE

How do I ride this?

1. At a medium trot on the circle, concentrate on achieving a truly round circle with your horse stepping over the exact center of each pole.

2. Ride both directions; your horse must remember to adjust his steps accurately while maintaining the bend.

3. As you and your horse become proficient, decrease the size of your circle.

Hint

Try placing a marker (a water bucket or even your trusty helper) at the center of your circle. To help you maintain exactly the same radius all the way around the circle, imagine a length of string connecting the circle is center to your knee. Keep this "string" taut all the way around the circle without breaking it.

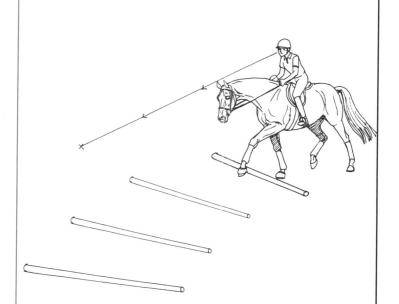

SETUP

Place ten to fifteen rails in various patterns around the ring. One quite complicated pattern you might set up is shown here, just one example of an infinite number of patterns you might create and ride. Incorporate any number of the preceding exercises in the patterns you devise.

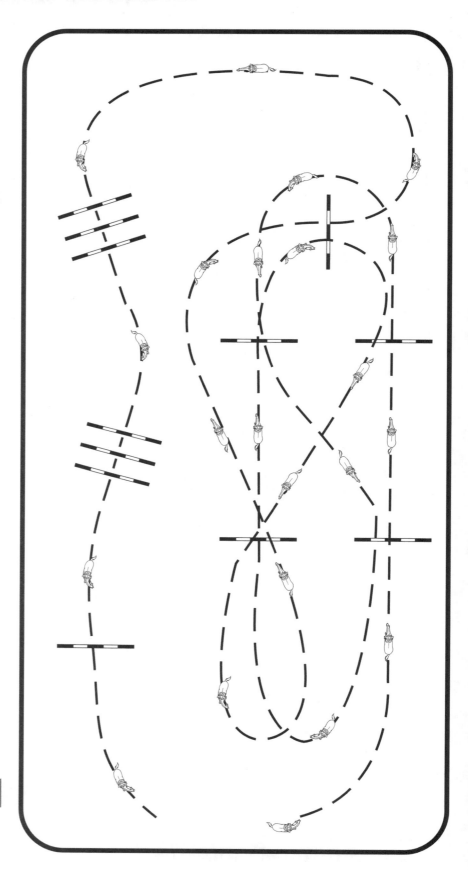

Key

Trot-pole ▬▬▬

Medium trot ─ ── ─ ──

A "Course" of Poles at the Trot

How do I ride this?

1. Memorize and ride the pattern.

2. Create either a shorter or longer "course" to ride.

3. Be precise about going straight, at an angle, approaching from a bend or circle, following with a bend, a circle, or a straight line throughout your course.

4. Ride a random pattern over the poles as part of your flatwork. Be sure to include many changes of direction.

Doublecheck

▶ Am I thinking ahead?
Make sure you keep your mind in front of your horse at all times. This is how you make the departure from one pole flow into the approach to the next. Flow is the secret to riding jumping courses well.

Benefits

This exercise presents an opportunity for you to practice your own "course designs" and challenges. It also develops your ability to "multi-task" — that is, to think about where you are going, how, and why, *and* to prepare yourself and your horse — all before the next rail is upon you.

> Flow *is the secret to riding jumping courses well.*

SETUP

Set a somewhat simpler pattern of poles in your arena than that in Exercise 23 (a sample is shown here; use your imagination to create others).

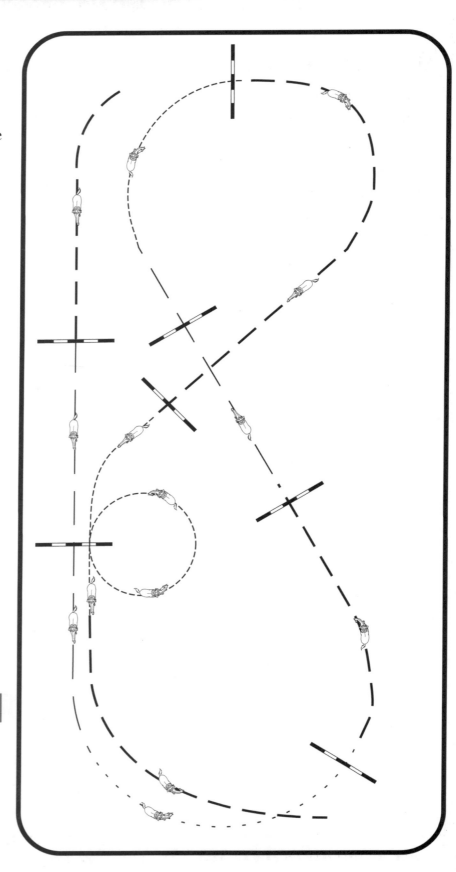

Key

Trot-pole ▬▭▬▭▬

Walk - - - - - -

Shortened trot - - - - - - - - -

Lengthened trot —— —— ——

Medium trot ▬▬ ▬▬ ▬▬

Random Rails with Changes in Stride

How do I ride this?

1. Follow the pattern indicated on the diagram or one that you have devised.

2. Ride the pattern in a variety of ways, including some approaches on angles and from the arc of a circle.

3. Alternate medium, long, and short stride work.

Doublecheck

▶ Am I making it very clear to my horse exactly what I expect and where?

▶ Are my transitions subtle, accurate, and prompt?

Reminders

▶ Avoid making any transitions (or changes to your plan) right in front of a pole.

▶ Always prepare for your line and stride well in advance.

SETUP

For this exercise, you will create interesting and challenging patterns even when using a few poles. One example is shown here.

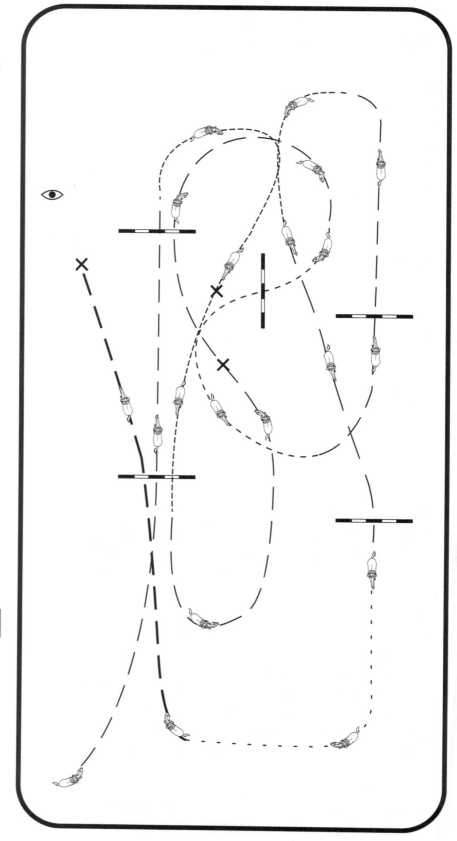

Key

Trot-pole ▬ ▬ ▬

Walk - - - - - - -

Lengthened trot —— —— ——

Medium trot ▬ ▬ ▬ ▬

Shortened trot - - - - - - - - - -

Halt ✗

Focal point ◉

RANDOM RAILS WITH HALTS AND CHANGES OF GAIT

How do I ride this?

1. Ride the pattern shown, including the transitions.

2. Create your own longer or shorter "course."

3. Work at both the trot and the walk, including some well-planned halts and transitions between the poles.

Doublecheck

▶ Are my horse and I concentrating throughout the course?

▶ Are our transitions smooth as well as accurate?

The longer your pattern and the greater the number and frequency of the transitions, the more challenging this is for both you and your horse. Your goal: Keep every transition smooth and accurate.

A CORRECT HALT

To achieve a correct halt the rider must be in a correct position *prior to* asking for the transition. Be sure you are in a full-seat position with your weight firmly in your heels, then square your shoulders and keep your upper body straight. Only after doing this should you close your fingers on the reins and say a quiet "Whoa." Persist until your horse is standing still — don't ever give up partway there. When you make a habit of preparing properly, your horse will learn to anticipate what comes next, making your job easier.

Am I ready for the next step?

▶ When you can combine the last three exercises and have fun "dancing" with your horse around the "ballroom" of your arena, it's time to move on to jumping.

▶ All the work that you've put into mastering ground poles makes the most difficult part of jumping courses — the part between the jumps — *so* much easier.

Let's begin with some basic gymnastic exercises that even a complete neophyte can use to successfully begin jumping.

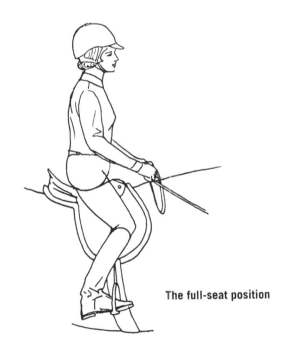

The full-seat position

Anne Kursinski on Eros.

TURNING POLES INTO JUMPS: GYMNASTICS

Gymnastic exercises from the trot are the classic method of introducing horses (and riders) to jumping. The first ones are very basic, taking one simple step at a time, and make a perfect start for even the greenest horse or rider. The simplest exercises can be used for improving the technique of a more advanced horse or to allow a more advanced rider to concentrate entirely on some aspect of their position.

Trot gymnastics also provide the first steps to cantering jumps consistently and quietly. While you will be entering each gymnastic line at the trot, your horse will naturally take canter strides after completing the first jump in the line. It is important that your horse continue to canter after the last fence in the line, coming quietly back to the trot when you ask him to.

If you are just beginning to jump you will need to pay special attention to your position. Assume your two-point position on the approach to the trot grid. Concentrate on sinking your weight into your heels, pressing your hands down onto your horse's neck, and keeping your head and focus up. In this secure position, relax sufficiently to feel your horse make the small jump over the first crossbar. Only after

your horse has continued two to three strides beyond the final obstacle in the line should you quietly resume your light seat and bring your horse back to the posting trot.

Releasing your hands and arms is important. You do not want to punish your horse — by catching him in the mouth — when he makes a good jumping effort! The moderate crest release is the first one to learn and the one every rider should use in gymnastic lines. Any rider whose lower leg is not totally secure (or whose horse tends to jump extra high or awkwardly on occasion) should learn to "pinch mane" at the jumps (see Exercise 26 for an explanation) while they work on their leg position and strength.

The height of the jumps you should use must be relative to the experience level of both you and your horse. Always begin very conservatively; have your helper handy to raise and/or spread the jumps a little at a time until an exercise feels a bit challenging but well within your capabilities. Consistency in your performance is what is important. Jumping is largely a matter of habit (for you and your horse); form good habits to get good results.

EXERCISE 26

SETUP

Set a grid of three or four trot-poles at your horse's optimal spacing for trot work. Double this distance from the last pole to a set of standards. Place two poles next to each other on the ground between them.

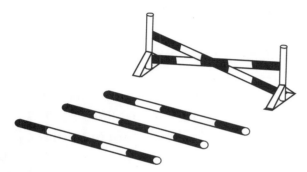

A simple "trot-in" gymnastic.

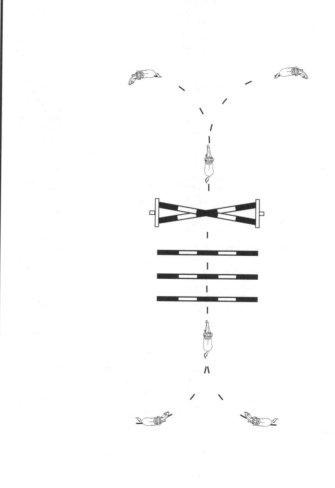

Key

Trot — – – – –

Trot-pole

Cross bar ⋈

THE MOST BASIC GYMNASTIC

How do I ride this?

1. Ride at a medium trot straight through the middle of the grid and over the two poles on the ground between the standards.

Inexperienced horses or riders should do this a couple of times before proceeding to the next step.

2. Raise the ends of the poles to form a cross bar approximately 12 in. (30cm) in the center.

3. Ride at a medium trot through the middle of the grid and over the cross bar.

PINCHING MANE

If you lack a secure leg or are riding a horse with a tendency to over-jump, master the technique of "pinching mane" so you won't catch him in the mouth by mistake. As your horse enters the trot-pole grid, soften your arms to allow your elbows to move forward. Press your hands firmly on the top of the horse's neck, about one-third of the distance between the withers and the ears. With one hand, pinch a substantial chunk of the horse's mane between your thumb and the knuckle of your forefinger. Practice on the flat first, so that this becomes a smooth and relaxed move that will become automatic should something unexpected happen.

Problem solving

▶ I'm feeling insecure or unbalanced when my horse makes a small jump over the cross bar.

Well in front of the trot-poles, establish an energetic, but not hurried, trot. Be sure your leg is positioned securely under you, with your weight into your heels. Keep your seat very light and your back relaxed. As you approach the poles focus on a point at the end of the arena beyond the cross bar. Now, just let your horse do the work while you enjoy the sensation of him jumping under you.

Benefits

▶ Repetition creates a relaxed, attentive horse. If your horse is stiff or tense, repetition will soon cause him to lower his head.

▶ Because the trot-poles create the same take-off point for the jump each and every time, this basic gymnastic encourages consistency in a horse's jumping. This makes it ideal for introducing jumping to a tentative or insecure rider.

Reminder

The point of cavalletti exercises is for each portion to lead the horse naturally into executing every subsequent segment naturally and accurately.

SETUP

Set a basic trot-pole grid, followed by a cross bar (the same as in Exercise 26.)

> *The accuracy of your aids and your horse's willingness to listen and cooperate are critical to smooth and accomplished riding.*

Reminder

Your ultimate objective is to ride effectively over entire courses of jumps. Since the departure from each jump can quickly become (or at least affect) the approach to the next one, it is vitally important to be just as effective and in control *after* a jump as *before* it.

This is achieved by *always* having a plan and some specific goal for both horse and rider to accomplish as they land and continue on.

The accuracy of your aids and your horse's willingness to listen and cooperate are critical to smooth and accomplished riding.

Key

Medium trot — — — — — —

Medium canter ▬▬ ▬ ▬ ▬▬ ▬

Simple change of lead ⊗

Trot-pole ▬▬▬▬

Cross bar ▷◁

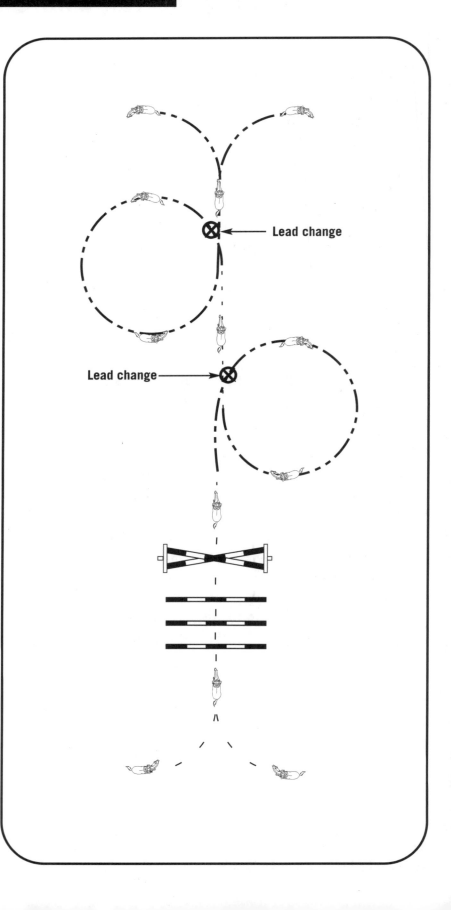

Lead change

Lead change

PLANNING YOUR START AND FINISH

How do I ride this?

Planning your start is fairly straightforward. Always have your rhythm established before you begin the turn into the line of jumps. If you need to circle to achieve rhythm, do so. By this time, you should be able to establish steady tempo within a half-circle.

A planned finish must be a part of even the most basic exercise. Your plan can have many variations. After riding through the gymnastic, start with simply completing a circle (called in the hunter ring your **closing circle**), alternating the direction each time. Generally, you want the last jump in the grid also to be the first **canter** stride for your finishing circle.

If you are a timid rider or riding a very green or hot horse, use the strides after the final pole or jump to complete a downward transition to a trot prior to beginning your closing circle.

Otherwise, continue in the canter, finishing your circle with a smooth and progressive downward transition through the trot into the walk, if you are finished, or into the trot to continue back through your grid. If your horse lands over the pole or jump on the incorrect lead for the circle you have planned, do a simple or **flying change** of lead *before* entering your closing circle.

When a single circle feels easy, add a **simple change** of lead followed by a second circle in the opposite direction.

> The start and finish are vital parts of every exercise.

Doublecheck

▶ Am I planning the next segment of the exercise while I ride?

You are now learning to do just that. The secret to a cooperative horse is a rider who gives clear directions in time for the horse to prepare both mentally and physically for whatever he is being asked to do.

Benefits

If your horse has developed the habit of **playing** or **scooting off** after a jump or a line of jumps, using a range of variations on this simple exercise is the most effective way of overcoming what can be an annoying and even dangerous trait.

SETUP

Start with the Basic Gymnastic (see Exercise 26).

For very green horses or timid riders, begin by setting this "jump" as two rails placed together on the ground between the standards.

Measure 18 ft (5.5m) straight ahead from the back of your cross bar and set up a second pair of jump standards.

NOTE: For most horses, a trot stride is approximately 4 ft., 6 in. (1.4m). It can vary, however, especially for ponies or horses with exceptionally short or long strides.

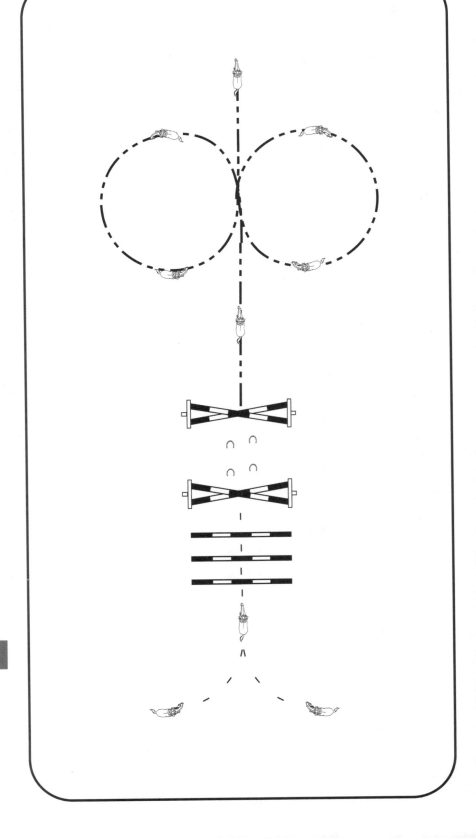

Key

Trot-pole	▬ ▬ ▬
Cross bar	▷◁
One canter stride	∩ ∩
Medium trot	— — — —
Medium canter	▬ ▬ ▬ ▬

BASIC GYMNASTIC PLUS A SECOND CROSS BAR

How do I ride this?

1. Trot straight through the line. Building from correct execution of Exercise 27, the additional jump follows naturally for even the greenest horse.

2. Maintain an even rhythm and a straight line. That's all!

Doublecheck

▸ Am I doing as little as possible?!

▸ Am I sinking my weight into my heels and keeping my focus up and ahead?

Benefits

▸ This is the most basic exercise for teaching a horse to prepare his balance in front of a jump and make any necessary adjustments to accommodate a minor misstep or being just a little too slow or fast before a jump.

▸ This exercise is excellent for the rider who tends to anticipate the jump or **duck** with the upper body.

▸ The opportunity this exercise offers for multiple repetitions is helpful in creating good habits — or overcoming bad ones.

Variations

The following variations improve security and feel for more advanced riders.

▸ More advanced riders should ride this exercise without irons and/or with their eyes closed.

▸ If a suitable confined area and supervision are available, riders should knot their reins and ride this with their arms held straight out from their sides.

SETUP

Start with the Basic Gymnastic with the cross bar from the previous exercise.

You can set your second obstacle as two poles on the ground or as a cross bar to begin this exercise, then convert it to a small vertical. To make a small vertical, place one of the cross poles horizontally in the jump cups and set the other as a ground line between 6 and 12 in. (15 to 30cm) in front.

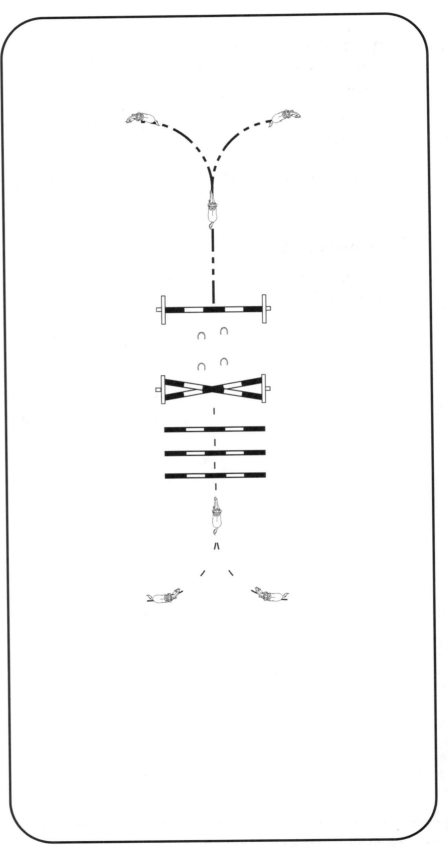

Key

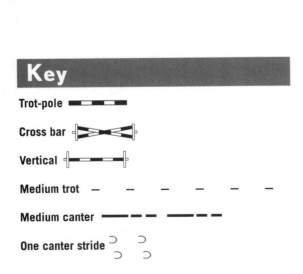

Trot-pole ▰▰▰

Cross bar ▷◁▷◁

Vertical ▭▬▭

Medium trot — — — — —

Medium canter ▬▬ ▬▬ ▬▬ ▬▬

One canter stride ⌒ ⌒ ⌒

BASIC GYMNASTIC PLUS A VERTICAL

How do I ride this?

1. Trot in, being sure to plan your start and finish.

2. Remain quiet with your body and allow your horse to figure out what to do. Be sure to release your hands as you did for the two-point position (described in Exercise 4).

Doublecheck

Am I quiet with my body and consistent with my aids?

A CROSS BAR OR A VERTICAL?

The first obstacle for horses or riders beginning to jump in an arena setting should be one of these two:

The **cross bar** has the advantage of encouraging the horse to seek the center of the jump. However, you must be careful not to place the two poles against each other. Should it be knocked by your horse, the front pole should not hit against the back pole before it can fall out of the way. Why scare (or punish) an inexperienced horse when he makes a "green" mistake? Keep your horse relaxed when you want him to learn.

A small **vertical**, with a ground line approximately 6 in. (15cm) in front, can be an alternative to a cross bar. A vertical can seem less intimidating to a "spooky" greenie. You need to take extra care to navigate over the center of the vertical.

SETUP

Using the setup from Exercise 28, add another set of standards 1 to 2 ft. (30 to 60cm) behind your second cross bar, as shown in the diagram.

After you trot through a time or two, have your helper add jump cups. Place a horizontal pole behind the **cross bar** approximately 6 in. (15cm) higher than the center of the crossed poles.

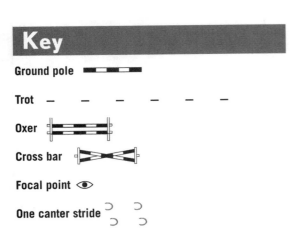

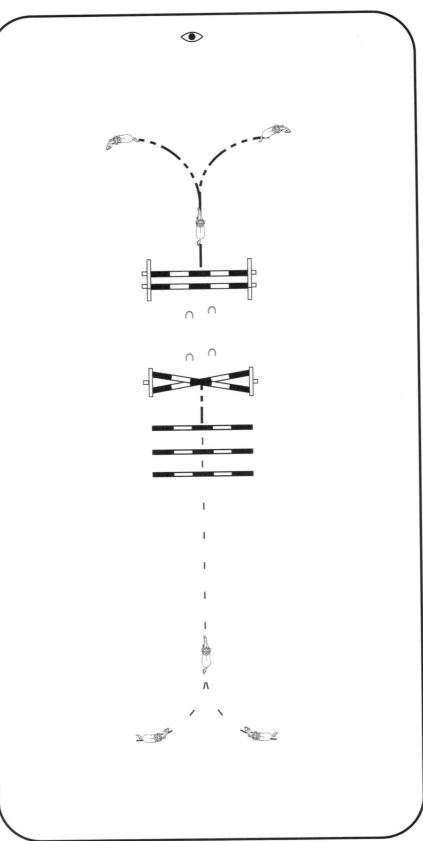

Key

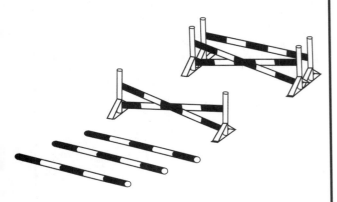

Ground pole	▬▬▬▬▬
Trot	— — — — —
Oxer	⊟
Cross bar	⋈
Focal point	👁
One canter stride	∪ ∪ ∪ ∪

INTRODUCING WIDTH

How do I ride this?

Trot in and ride straight toward a focal point at the far end of the arena.

Reminders

▶ Keep everything quiet, calm, and understated.

▶ Give your horse a little support with your leg.

▶ Look up and ride toward your focal point at the end of the ring. This is especially important on horses with a tendency to jump higher when the jump has an element of width.

Benefits

It is as important that a horse knows how to handle an obstacle's width as its height. With a very green horse, begin using oxers quite early on, and use them throughout their training along with vertical jumps. Keep the width in proportion to the height — from 3 to 6 in. (5 to 15cm) more width than height — is a good rule of thumb for Show Jumping.

WHAT IF MY HORSE "STALLS IN THE AIR" OVER A SPREAD?

Occasionally a horse jumps too much "up" rather than "across" when encountering a **spread** jump. Whether it is a young horse's confusion about how to handle a new type of jump or a more experienced horse making a rare mistake, it is important not to let this experience leave a bad memory in his mind.

The use of **safety cups** (special cups that release the pole when a horse exerts downward pressure on it) to hold the back poles of spread jumps is highly recommended. If unavailable, the next best choice is very shallow cups that won't hold the pole too securely.

If all you have available are the common, deeper jump cups, have your helper **lip the cup** for safety. Simply balance the pole on the *back edge* of the cup rather than down in the bottom of it. This permits the pole to fall if **rubbed** lightly, preventing your horse from pulling over the whole standard in the event of a serious mistake.

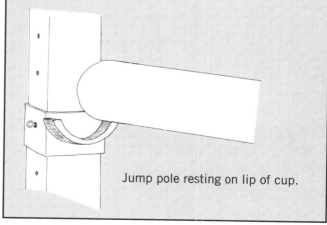

Jump pole resting on lip of cup.

SETUP

To the Basic Gymnastic (followed by a vertical) in Exercise 29, add a back rail to the vertical jump to create a small oxer.

Start with it quite narrow and keep the ground line a little closer than for the vertical.

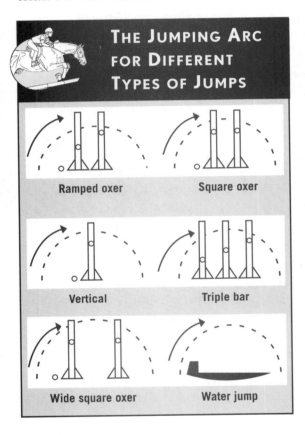

THE JUMPING ARC FOR DIFFERENT TYPES OF JUMPS

Ramped oxer

Square oxer

Vertical

Triple bar

Wide square oxer

Water jump

Key

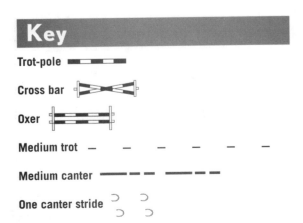

Trot-pole

Cross bar

Oxer

Medium trot

Medium canter

One canter stride

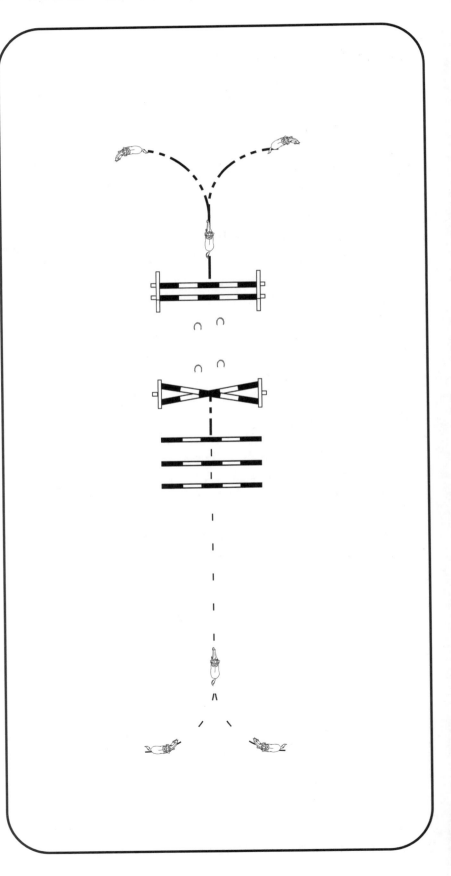

BASIC GYMNASTIC PLUS AN OXER

How do I ride this?

Your ride should be identical to the previous exercise.

Note that in these exercises, a cross bar is the initial jumping element of the gymnastic. (More experienced horses and riders can replace this with a small or moderate vertical.) An oxer may also serve as the first jumping effort in the gymnastic, although it is not recommended until both you and your horse are very consistent in your approach through the trot-poles. When you reach this stage of proficiency, reduce the distance from the trot-pole to the jump up to 1 ft. (30cm) to accommodate the width of the spread.

Problem solving

▶ How high can I jump from the trot?

Horses can easily jump quite large fences from the trot — some are very good at it, in fact. It is the rider that finds it more difficult, since the thrust off the ground may loosen the position of any rider lacking in strong basics.

JUMPING ARCS

A ramped oxer is one built with the front rail lower than the back rail. This ascending shape is easier for a horse to jump without rubbing the front pole, since he can afford to be a little bit slower lifting his front legs. It encourages a horse to stretch out his arc over the jump. This type of oxer is best to use when first introducing horses to spreads. Limit the height difference between front and back poles to 3 to 6 in. (5 to 15cm). Notice the difference in the arc taken by a horse over the two types of oxers as shown in the diagram above, as well as what is necessary for vertical jumps, triple bars, wide oxers, and water jumps. Each one requires a horse to balance his jumping arc over the highest portion of the jump. Verticals and narrow, ascending oxers give the most leeway in take-off point, while wide spreads need to be negotiated from a more precise spot if the jumping effort is to be successful.

Bear in mind that the horse's balance and impulsion are at least as important as the take-off point. A horse's jumping experience and how much his rider helps (or hinders) him with his task also have a lot to do with his "comfort range."

Rider showing a balanced, secure, and relaxed position over a larger oxer.

SETUP

Start with your Basic Gymnastic plus vertical (see Exercise 29). Measure from your final obstacle to an additional pair of standards to add another jump to your line.

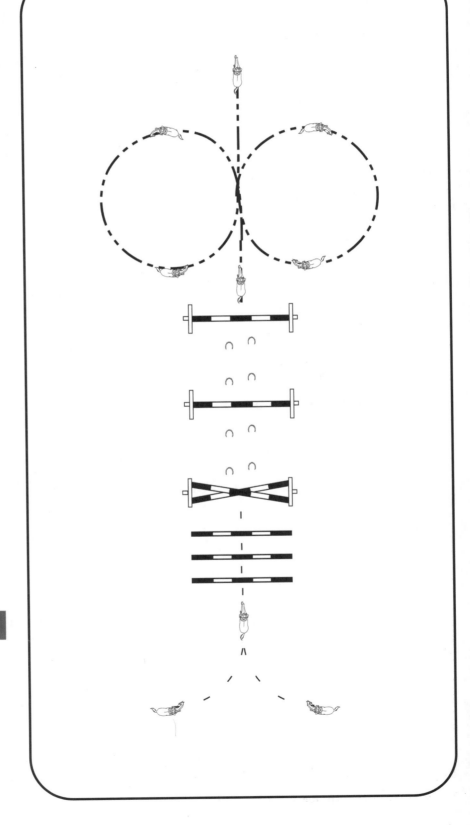

Key

Trot	– – – – –
One canter stride	◠ ◠ / ◠ ◠
Canter	— – — – — –
Trot-pole	▬▬▬
Cross bar	◸◿
Vertical	▯▬▬▬▯

Basic Gymnastic plus Vertical to Vertical

How do I ride this?

Trot through the exercise. Remember to land over the initial jump in a canter and maintain your impulsion and rhythm through the rest of the line.

Doublecheck

▶ Am I sitting still, in the center of my horse, with my eyes up?

These gymnastic exercises are a primary learning tool for the horse. Their benefit comes from allowing a horse to become comfortable and expert at balancing the take-off stride.

This is achieved only when you remain as quiet and out of your horse's way as possible. This is his opportunity to figure things out — let him do it on his own!

Benefits

Depending on subtle variations in the distances set, the size of the jumps, and the ground line distances used, a horse can be encouraged to lengthen or compress his stride, as well as to speed up his technique with his front legs.

By gradually adjusting the distances you set, you help your horse learn how to accomplish far more than what comes naturally to him right now.

MORE ON DISTANCES

In gymnastic exercises, the basic one-stride distance from the first trot jump to the next jump is 18 ft. (5.5m) and from the second canter jump to another jump is 20 to 21 ft. (6 to 6.3m) for most horses. Keep in mind what you already know about your horse's natural stride length when setting this exercise for the first time.

Most important at the beginning is to use distances that make your horse comfortable when executing the number of strides desired. If your horse needs to hurry, or is forced to take an awkwardly short stride to fit, your distances need fine-tuning.

SETUP

Using the setup from the previous exercise, add another pair of standards and a rail behind your final vertical to make an oxer.

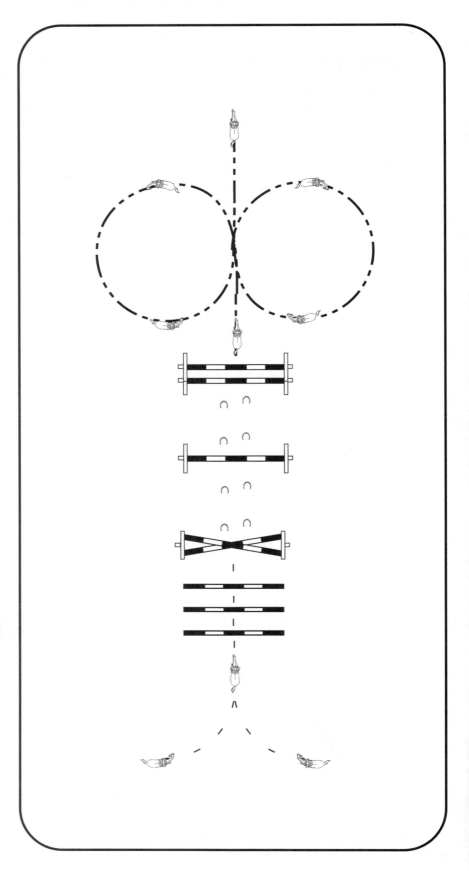

Key

Trot — – – – – –

One canter stride

Canter ▬ ▬ ▬ ▬ ▬

Trot-pole ▬▭▬

Cross bar ▷◁

Vertical ▬▭▬

Oxer ▭

BASIC GYMNASTIC PLUS VERTICAL TO OXER

How do I ride this?

Trot through the exercise. Remember to maintain your impulsion through the line.

Doublecheck

▶ Am I relaxed, with my eyes up, letting my horse execute the jumps without any interference on my part?

Reminder

▶ By this time, your horse will be comfortable jumping the oxer coming out of this line. He may also pay less attention to you after the line, or even want to "play" upon landing. This is the time when finishing each exercise is especially important (see Exercise 27).

SQUARE OXER

A square oxer — one where the front and back rails are set at the same height — requires a horse to execute a correct arc over the jump. When little or no ground line is used with a square oxer, even the experienced horse needs to be very quick and accurate in judging the size and location of the top poles, front and back. This makes the square oxer the best choice for more experienced jumpers in most schooling situations.

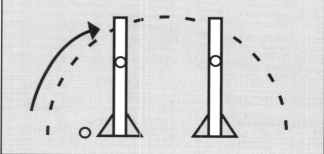

SETUP

If you are beginning with the setup in Exercise 31, measure 21 to 22 ft. (6.40 to 6.70m) to allow one stride following the oxer and build a vertical jump.

If you are setting this exercise after jumping Exercise 33, first set the oxer and then measure from it to position the vertical correctly.

NOTE: Whenever changing any vertical to an oxer in the middle of a line of jumps, you must re-measure for the jumps that follow the newly constructed oxer. This is necessary to accommodate the oxer's width and assure your horse has the correct distance between each jump.

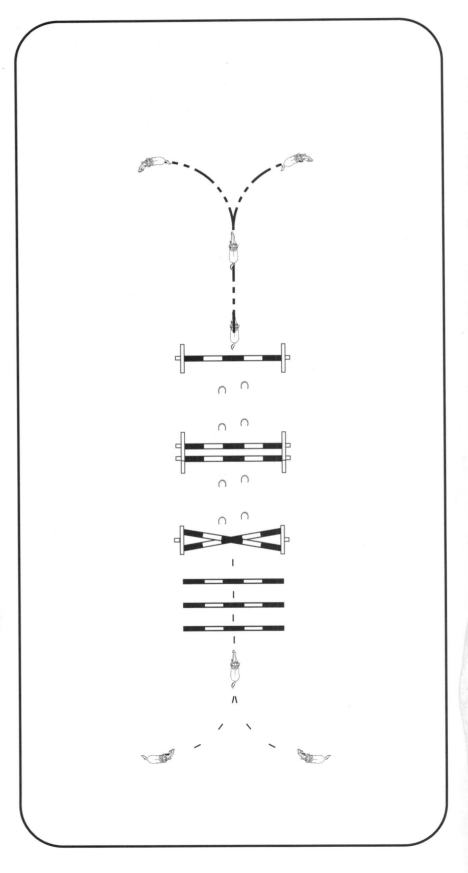

Key

Trot	— — — — — —
One canter stride	
Medium canter	— — — — — —
Trot-pole	▬▬▬
Cross bar	▷◁
Vertical	⊣▐▐▐⊢
Oxer	▬▬▬

BASIC GYMNASTIC PLUS OXER TO VERTICAL

How do I ride this?

Trot through the exercise. Remember to finish the exercise with a closing circle and a smooth transition back to the trot.

Doublecheck

▶ Am I quiet and centered, giving my horse the chance to balance himself before the final vertical?

If you are a rider who needs more work on position in order to be really solid, having this fence after the oxer is good practice.

Benefits

Depending on subtle variations in the distances used, as well as the size and shape of the jumps, this exercise can improve your horse's balance and teach him not to lengthen his stride as he goes through the line.

OXERS AFFECT DISTANCES

In jumping lines, oxers change the way your distances ride. Generally a lower, ramped oxer puts a horse on a slightly longer stride upon landing. To handle a short distance, a taller vertical, or a square oxer after a ramped spread, your horse needs to be better balanced and more clever. Avoid making your test too difficult until your horse has the experience to handle it.

EXERCISE 35

SETUP

Adding to the setup for Exercise 34, place another set of standards behind your final vertical and create a second oxer.

If you are progressing from Exercise 31, have your helper measure to and set the additional jump.

USING A "CLUCK"

Many experienced jumping riders make good use of the clucking sound made by pulling the tongue away from the inside of the cheek. Most horses naturally interpret this sharp sound as a signal to go forward. An audible aid such as this has two very big advantages: It is always instantly available and does not require you to make any potentially distracting change in balance or position.

Using a strong leg aid at the jump can weaken your leg position. Leaning ahead just before take-off won't make your horse go forward, and will abruptly change your horse's balance — just at the worst possible moment. Learn to use a quick cluck when your horse needs encouragement.

Key

Trot-pole

Cross bar

Oxer

Medium trot — — — — — —

Medium canter — — — — — —

One canter stride

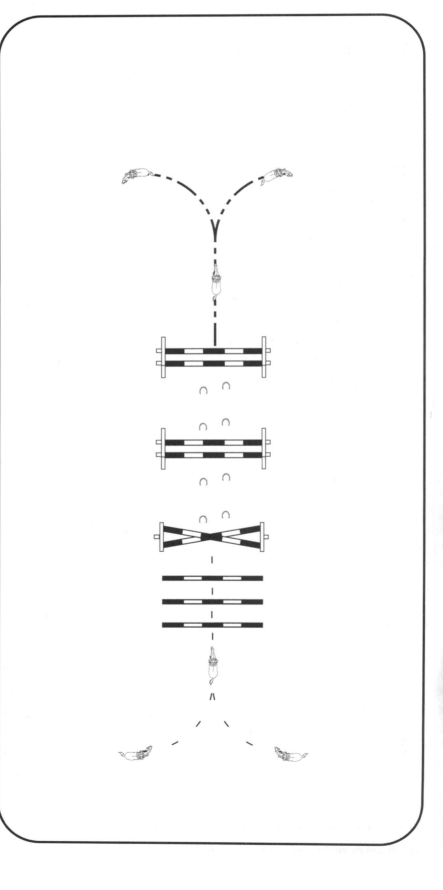

BASIC GYMNASTIC PLUS OXER TO OXER

How do I ride this?

Trot through this grid, remembering impulsion, balance, rhythm, and your opening and closing circles.

Doublecheck

▶ Do I have enough impulsion and balance to ride all the way through this?

Jumping multiple spread fences in succession always requires a great deal more effort from your horse (along with more security in your own position).

Landing off the first oxer without good impulsion and balance makes the second one more difficult.

If your horse requires a little encouragement to go forward when landing or taking off from a jump, a "cluck" is a valuable aid.

TEACHING YOUR HORSE TO RESPOND TO A CLUCK

If your horse doesn't respond to a cluck by moving immediately and energetically forward, teach him what it means during a warm-up for a jumping session.

In the trot, give a single cluck and ask for an immediate upward transition into a strong canter with your aids. If your horse is slow to respond, use your spur briefly and strongly to back up your aids. Once your horse is going forward energetically, quietly come back to the trot, and repeat.

Do this several times until your horse is anticipating what is to come and goes right into the canter on that first cluck. Then, see if your horse will move into a canter without hesitation from the walk, reinforcing your normal aids with a cluck.

With some very lazy horses, it might require one or more strong lessons. If necessary, use your stick (quickly and smartly, one or two times immediately behind your leg) to achieve the response you are looking for. Use the stick as a way to surprise your horse into giving you the immediate depart into the more forward gait — not as a punishment. It is easy to get left "in the back seat" when your horse responds correctly and moves forward quickly, so anticipate his response and be careful not to punish him with your hands for doing the right thing.

Be sure to reward your horse when he moves forward, and be especially soft and quiet as you return to the slower gait. Use repetition and determination until your horse clearly understands that his response to the cluck must *always* be to go forward — right now!

SETUP

Add an additional vertical jump to the setup you used in Exercise 32, setting the same distance to the third vertical as for the first two.

NOTE: Repeating your basic distance is fine as long as the obstacles are low. However, when asking your horse to jump a bit higher, it might be best to provide your horse with approximately 1 ft. (30cm) additional distance toward the end of higher, longer gymnastic lines.

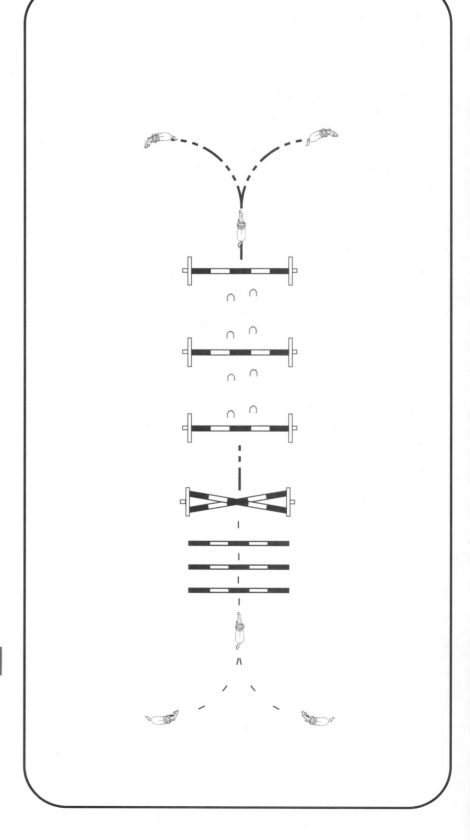

Key

Trot-pole

Vertical

Cross bar

Medium trot —   —   —   —   —   —

Medium canter ▬ ▬▬ ▬ ▬▬ ▬

BASIC GYMNASTIC plus THREE VERTICALS

How do I ride this?

Ride this the same way you have been riding the previous exercises.

Problem solving

▶ My horse is stalling in the line.

You may need to support your horse a bit more with your leg, maintaining a quiet upper body, as you raise the fences to a more challenging height.

As the gymnastics become more challenging, consistent focus, a quiet and strong riding position, and greater impulsion from your horse become critical.

Benefits

Gymnastics consisting of multiple jumps in a straight line, with the basic trot-in as the setup, remain the most classic and effective method for perfecting a horse's jumping technique.

WHY MORE JUMPS IN A GYMNASTIC?

When you add jumps to the line, your horse must work harder to keep his balance and maintain his concentration throughout. In these exercises your horse learns to engage his hindquarters and lighten his front end. He becomes adept at correcting any mistakes he might have made the last time through.

Two secrets to using gymnastic lines most effectively are:

1. Customize the distances and the size and shape of the jumps to teach your horse how to handle with confidence almost any question put to him.

2. Ride well enough to stay out of your horse's way while he learns.

You will need an arena at least 200 ft. (60m) long to ride a longer exercise comfortably. Always provide enough room for your approach and departure. An absolute minimum of 50 ft. (15m) from the end of your arena is necessary.

The next exercises illustrate most of the various basic jump combinations.

SETUP

Move your extra standards behind the final vertical from Exercise 36 to turn it into an oxer.

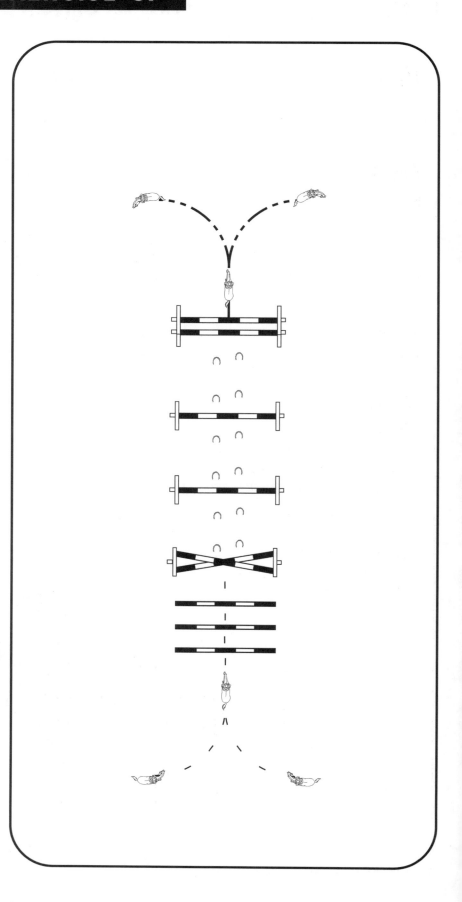

Key

Trot — – — – — –

One canter stride

Medium canter —— – – — – —

Trot-pole

Cross bar

Vertical

Oxer

BASIC GYMNASTIC PLUS VERTICAL – VERTICAL – OXER

How do I ride this?

Trot into this line. Your ride remains identical to the previous exercises.

Doublecheck

▶ Am I sitting quietly in the center of my horse, with my eyes up?

▶ Am I staying with the horse's motion and center of gravity?

▶ Do I have enough impulsion?

▶ Am I falling back too soon, thus impeding my horse's jumping arc over the oxer?

Benefits

This particular line of jumps asks the horse to roll back onto his hindquarters twice over verticals before ending the line with an extension out over the oxer.

It emphasizes the importance of patience in the early part of a line, while maintaining sufficient impulsion to finish across the width of the spread.

HOW HORSES JUMP VERTICALS VS. OXERS

As you utilize these gymnastics to jump higher, wider, and more difficult sequences of obstacles, you will find that the verticals are most useful for creating a tighter and more elevated jumping arc. The oxers teach your horse to jump up higher than the actual measured height of the obstacle, creating an arc that allows him to clear both front and back rails.

SETUP

If you build this exercise from Exercise 33 (Vertical to Oxer), measure, then add a final vertical.

If you build this from Exercise 37, the distances between the jumps must be re-measured and set accurately. Remember, when creating an oxer as a middle jump in the line, the width of the oxer must be taken into account.

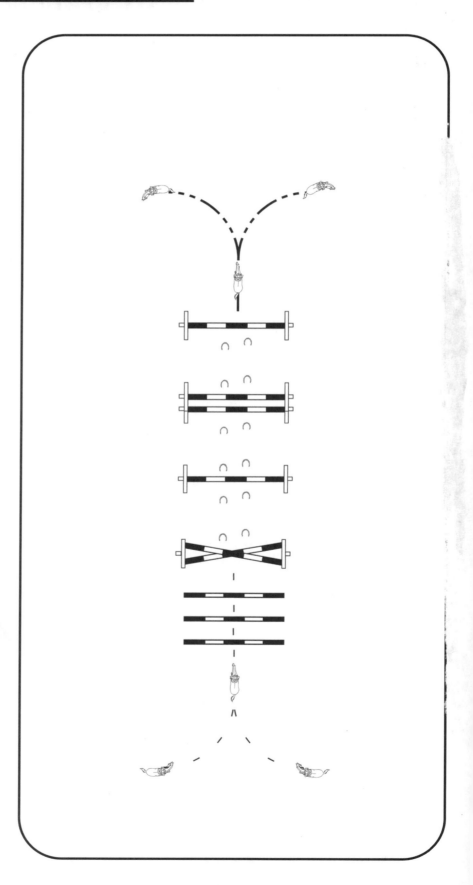

Key

Trot	— – – – – —
One canter stride	⌒ ⌒ ⌒ ⌒
Medium canter	— – — – —
Trot-pole	▬▭▬
Cross bar	▷◁
Vertical	├─▭─┤
Oxer	▬▬

BASIC GYMNASTIC PLUS VERTICAL – OXER – VERTICAL

How do I ride this?

Trot into the line. Your ride remains identical to the previous exercises.

Doublecheck

▶ Am I sitting quietly in the center of my horse with my focus up?

▶ Am I staying with the horse's motion and secure over each fence?

▶ Do I have enough impulsion for the spread and a compressed horse for the vertical?

Benefits

This exercise helps your horse learn to create the right shape over a variety of jumps and to quickly adapt his arc when going from one type of jump to another.

It is important for you to remember to use your balance to assist your horse. Wait with your upper body as you approach the final vertical; shifting your balance forward, even a touch ahead of your horse, makes his job much harder.

WHAT ABOUT WIDER OXERS?

As soon as you and your horse are ready, you need to begin training with wider oxers, especially if your horse is destined to become a jumper. Width affects the distances and how they ride. A short distance before an oxer requires your horse to be both quicker with his front legs and more powerful in his back in order to jump across the width. A vertical following an oxer demands that your horse return to a tighter arc after stretching across the spread.

EXERCISE 39

SETUP

Starting from the setup for Exercise 38, change the first fence to an oxer, the middle to a vertical, and the final one to an oxer.

Remember to re-measure your distances carefully, since you are changing one of your middle jumps from a vertical to an oxer (see Setup in Exercise 38).

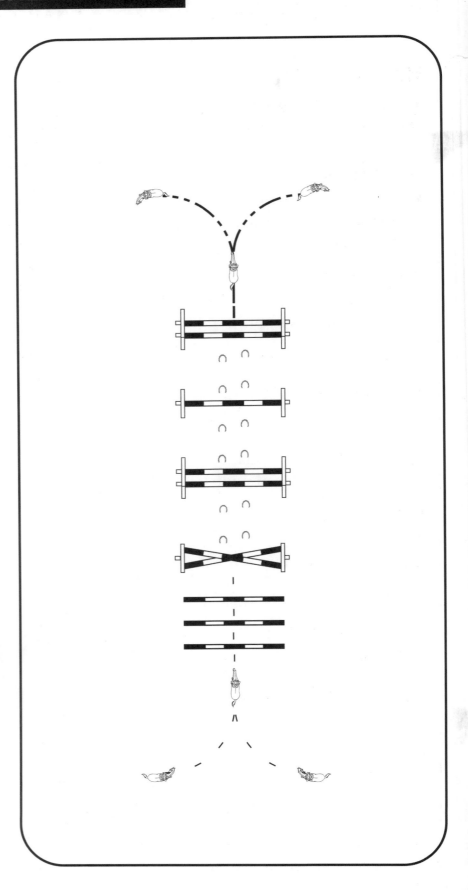

Key

Trot — – – – –

One canter stride

Medium canter — – – – –

Trot-pole ▬▬▬

Cross bar ▷◁

Vertical |▬▬|

Oxer ▬ ▬

Basic Gymnastic plus Oxer – Vertical – Oxer

How do I ride this?

Trot into the line. Your ride remains identical to the previous exercises.

Doublecheck

▶ Is my horse still attentive to my aids after this line of jumps so my finish is controlled and smooth?

▶ Are the multiple spread jumps loosening my position resulting in my lower leg slipping back?

▶ Am I able to remain quiet with my upper body?

▶ Have I established sufficient impulsion in my horse's trot when entering the line?

Hint

Two spreads within a line always require more impulsion and power from your horse. The vertical in the middle means you must also allow your horse time to rebalance and shorten his jumping arc.

USING THE RIGHT GYMNASTIC

If you are using gymnastics for the wonderful opportunity they offer for you to work on the fine points of your position and balance, it is a good idea to practice over many different kinds. Variety is good for your progress.

Using gymnastics for educating your horse, on the other hand, requires careful consideration of your horse's particular strengths and weaknesses. Notice what he does easily and which errors he is prone to make. Then choose the exercises that give him the best practice and experience with which to gain confidence in dealing with a variety of problems.

SETUP

Build this exercise from Exercise 33 (Vertical – Oxer) and 38 (Vertical – Oxer – Vertical), using small, ramped oxers, and comfortable distances.

NOTE: When using square oxers built higher and wider, this becomes a difficult exercise. Negotiating two spreads following a vertical requires a great deal of impulsion and power from your horse.

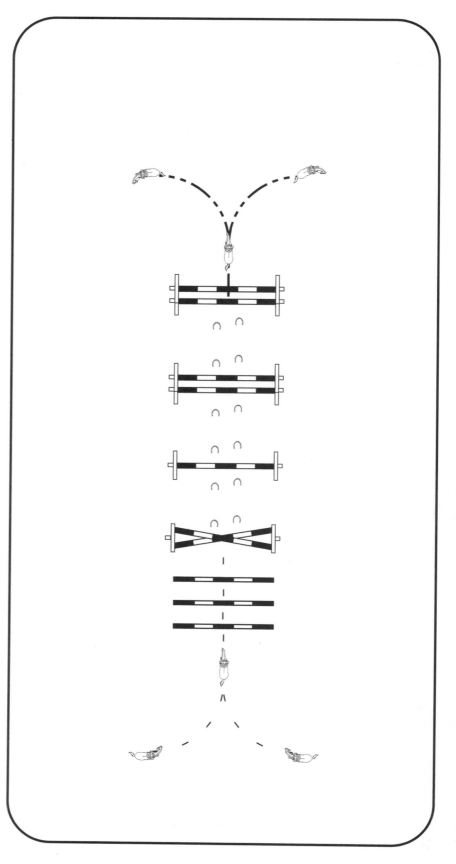

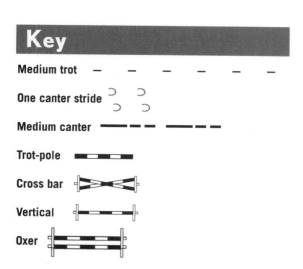

Key

Medium trot — — — — — —

One canter stride

Medium canter ━ ━ ━ ━ ━ ━

Trot-pole

Cross bar

Vertical

Oxer

BASIC GYMNASTIC PLUS VERTICAL – OXER – OXER

How do I ride this?

Trot into the line. Your ride remains identical to the previous exercises.

> *Your approach has more impact on a jump's difficulty than its height or width.*

Benefits

Small, ramped oxers and comfortable distances encourage your horse and help him develop a more positive, forward attitude.

Reminders

▶ A longer gymnastic series, especially one containing multiple spread jumps, can quickly become a real challenge for many horses, even over moderate-sized jumps.

▶ Make haste slowly!

▶ Use your ground person as your "mirror" to help you evaluate both your horse's and your own progress. Are you becoming the balanced and quiet rider that provides your horse with the best opportunity to learn and execute properly?

HOW HIGH SHOULD I BE JUMPING?

Every horse and rider benefit from training over a broad spectrum of jumps. You will come to understand that your approach has far more impact on a jump's difficulty than its height or width. Whatever height you are currently comfortable with over a complete course, you should feel confident jumping at least 6 in. (15cm) higher and wider whenever the approach is simplified, as it is in a gymnastic line.

Gymnastics set at comfortable distances are a perfect way to raise your sights and build your confidence. It is important to believe you can jump more than some arbitrary height. Today's limits are only a reflection of the training, experience, and natural talents of your horse.

A wise old horseman once said that a rider can always ride as fast as his horse can gallop: similarly, a rider can jump as high as his horse can jump. Belief in yourself, along with solid basics, are what make it possible.

Linda Allen on Iko.

GYMNASTICS WITH VARYING STRIDES

Gymnastics can be set using an almost infinite variety of distances. The next five exercises offer you many different possibilities. This Distance Chart provides distances suitable for the number of strides indicated.

The precise distance to use for your horse will depend on a variety of factors:

1. your horse's size and natural stride length;
2. his level of training, experience, and confidence;
3. what you are trying to accomplish in this particular training session.

Distance Chart

Number of strides between jumps.

This chart provides minimum and maximum distances between obstacles for the indicated number of strides, depending on the gait or previous jump. These distances will suit most horses.

Pole Placement	Bounce (no-stride)	1 Stride	2 Strides	3 Strides	4 Strides	5 Strides
Trot-poles	4'6"–4'9" 1.35–1.45m	9'–9'6" 2.75–2.90m	—	—	—	—
Canter poles	7'–8' 2.10–2.50m	14'–16' 4.20–5m	—	—	—	—
Placing pole at trot	7'–9' 2.10–2.75m	—	—	—	—	—
Placing pole at canter	8'6"–10' 2.60–3m	—	—	—	—	—
From a trot jump	9'6"–10'6 2.90–3.20m	18'–20' 5.50–6.10m	28'–30' 8.50–9.15m	39'–43' 12.00–13.10m	—	—
From a canter jump (in gymnastic)	10'–11'6" 3–3.50m	19'–22' 5.80–6.70m	30'–33' 9.15–10.05m	41'–45' 12.50–13.70m	52'–57' 15.90–17.40m	63'–68' 19.20–20.70m
Competition distance at 12' (3.66m) stride	—	24'–25' 7.30–7.60m	35'–36' 10.60–11m	48' 14.60m	60' 18.30m	72' 22m

TWO TO ONE TO THREE

Setting more complex grids

As you progress to more complex lines, begin each schooling session with the Basic Gymnastic (see Exercise 26) and add obstacles as your horse warms up. Even with a more experienced horse, always start with small jumps. As you add jumps to a line or raise or spread the obstacles, have your ground person watch your horse travel through the line and make any necessary adjustments to distances. Proper training is your goal; use your measuring tape to help you achieve it.

Gymnastics can be set with as many as six to eight jumps in a line. However, be sure not to set your entrance or exit from the line too close to the ends of your arena. A good rule of thumb is at least 60 ft. (18.30m), with an absolute minimum of 48 ft. (14.50m).

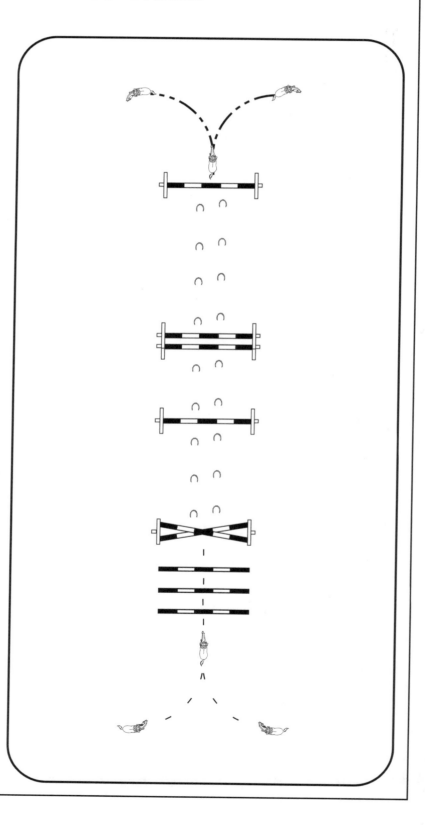

Key

Trot — — — — — —

One canter stride ⌒ ⌒

Medium canter ▬ ▬ ▬ ▬ ▬

BOUNCE TO ONE TO TWO TO ONE

What distances should I set?

Setting the appropriate distances for gymnastic training depends on your particular horse. Few 12·2-hand ponies can handle a distance that's right for a 17-hand horse! Some horses are also just more comfortable on a longer or shorter stride, or tend to jump with a bigger or smaller arc.

It is important when starting out to set your gymnastics to achieve even, consistent strides between the fences. Take-off and landing spots should be at nearly equal distances from the front and back of each jump. Have your ground person watch and comment.

After your horse maintains a consistent rhythm, gradually adjust the distances you use in order to teach him how to lengthen or shorten his stride when necessary.

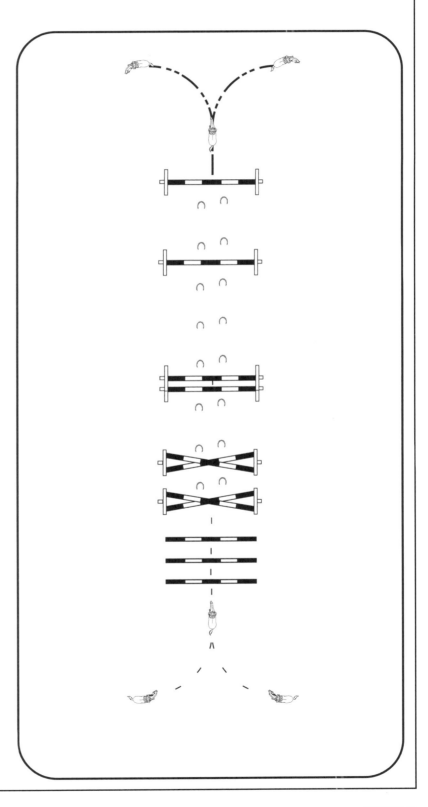

Key

Medium trot   —   —   —   —   —   —

Single canter stride (bounce)

Medium canter   —   —   —   —   —

One canter stride

Trot   —   —   —   —   —   —

Two to Three

My horse's stride isn't very long

Even short-strided horses can learn how to cover more ground on a jumping course. You, the rider, must teach this skill. If your horse hesitates to lengthen his stride to full length, begin with the stride that is comfortable for your horse and *gradually* lengthen the distances and/or increase the width of your spreads. In this way, your horse learns how to adapt his stride and his jumping arc and develop the confidence to do so whenever necessary.

A tense and nervous horse takes shorter and more rapid strides, resembling a sewing machine in high gear, defeating your whole purpose. Keep the exercises calm and relaxed, maintaining an even rhythm that encourages your horse to stretch and lengthen his stride rather than speed up.

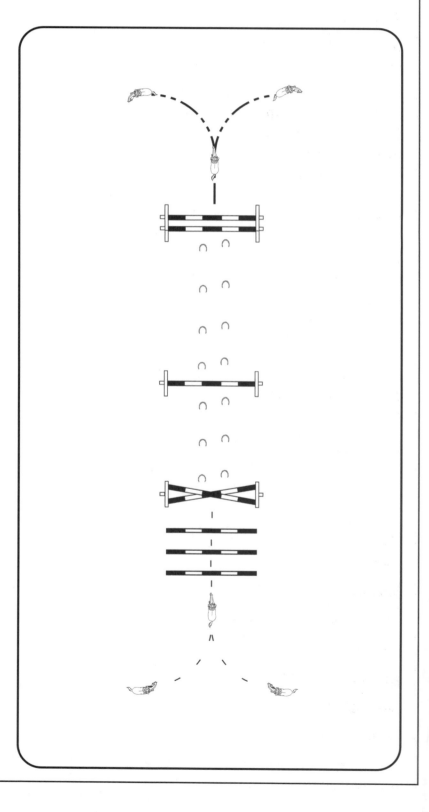

Key

Medium trot	— — — — —
One canter stride	∪ ∪
Medium canter	— – – – –

TWO TO TWO TO ONE

Know where you're headed!

While these variations can be very effective in establishing a consistent and confident approach to jumping, in order to achieve real success it is also essential to have your goals clearly in mind. Learn your horse's weak points and choose exercises to strengthen these areas. For example, Exercise 44 will remind the naturally forward horse to remain balanced and focused. The single stride to a vertical fence, after two stretching efforts, will require both collection and balance.

> *To achieve real success, it is essential to have your goals clearly in mind.*

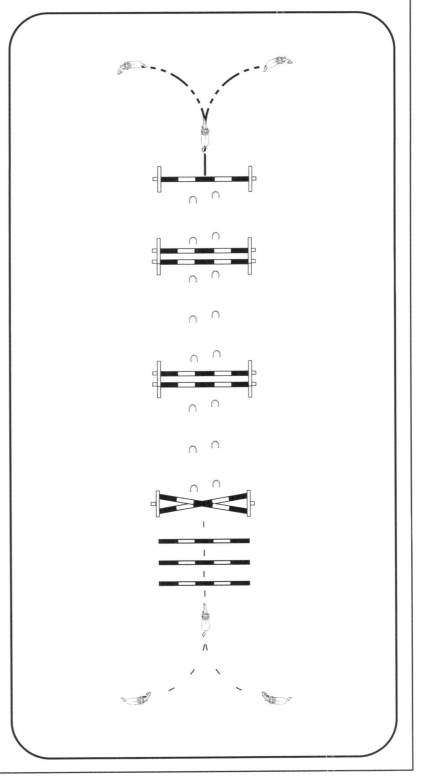

Key

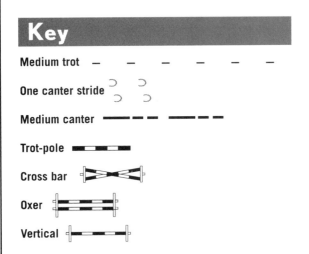

Medium trot   —   —   —   —

One canter stride

Medium canter   — — — — —

Trot-pole

Cross bar

Oxer

Vertical

GROUND POLES BETWEEN JUMPS

This type of an exercise, with a jump or a ground pole at nearly every stride, requires a horse to remain focused on where he is placing his feet at every step. A well-balanced horse can make a line like this look simple, neither gaining nor losing speed or impulsion from start to finish. Use low jumps. Start with fewer elements and add more as you become more proficient.

JUMPER, EVENTER, OR HUNTER . . .

Any of the exercises we have used so far can be utilized (at least in a simple form) for any jumping horse, no matter his "specialty." All horses will benefit from beginning their training over jumps with a very thorough grounding in gymnastic work. Jumpers and eventers build strength, gain confidence, and learn to adjust their stride and balance, while hunters improve technique and cadence. Gymnastic exercises properly tailored to the horse's needs always offer excellent refresher courses for even the most experienced jumpers.

Key

Medium trot — — — — —

Single canter stride (bounce)

One canter stride

Medium canter ▬ ▬ ▬ ▬ ▬

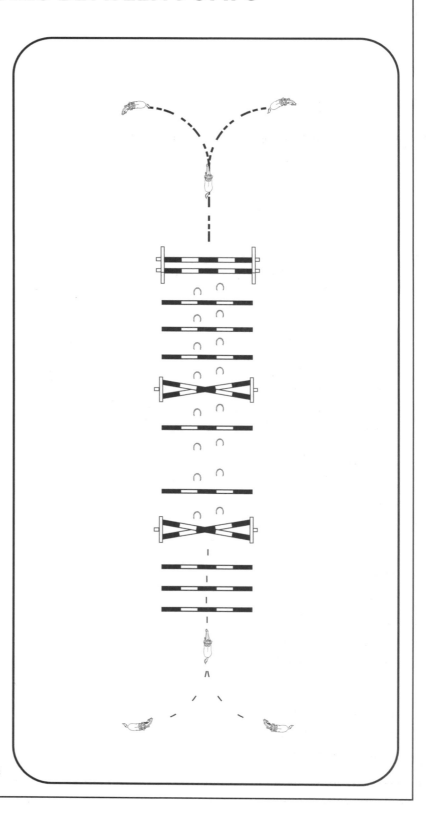

"SHORTCUT" GYMNASTIC

Setup

▶ Use the basic gymnastic from Exercise 26 and remove all but the final trot-pole that precedes the introductory cross rail (A).

▶ Once you are secure with riding the line, replace the cross bar with a small to moderate vertical (B).

▶ Finally, build the vertical into a small oxer. Remember to reduce the distance between the placing pole and the front of the oxer just a little because you are adding width to the jump (C).

How do I ride this?

1. Be sure your horse is traveling in a relaxed, rhythmic trot, just as he was when approaching the earlier exercises with the full grid.

2. With only one pole to prepare, achieving proper balance, cadence, and impulsion is going to depend to a much higher degree on your riding skill.

Doublecheck

▶ Is my horse awake and eager, in a steady and relaxed rhythm?

Learn to create impulsion, without adding speed or too much stride length.

▶ Can I remain balanced if my horse makes a last-minute adjustment to his step to accommodate the placing pole, so that a good take-off is achieved anyway?

It is important to feel your horse's gait under you. Only by sitting quietly is this possible.

Benefits

Trotting grids are invaluable to the training process; they establish the right habits in both horse and rider. The real test of the training is being able to achieve the same result without them.

When you are proficient over a single jump, use the placing pole as your entry into other, more complex gymnastics.

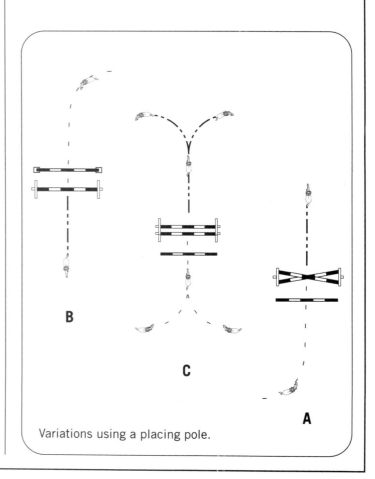

Variations using a placing pole.

SETUP

▶ Using the basic setup from Exercise 26, add two sets of standards off of the center line as shown in the diagram.

▶ Measure from the center of your first cross rail to the center of each of the two new angled jumps, setting the one-stride distance that fit your horse for Exercise 28.

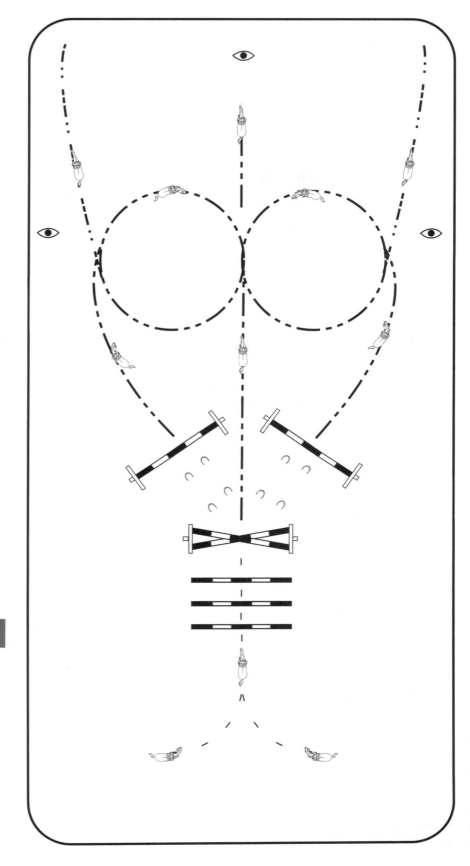

Key

Medium trot	— – – – – —
One canter stride	ͻ ͻ ͻ
Medium canter	—— – – —— –
Focal point	◉
Trot-pole	▬▬▬
Cross bar	◁▷
Vertical	◁▬▬▬▷

Basic Gymnastic in a "Y"

How do I ride this?

1. Trot straight into the exercise, planning which of the two final jumps, left or right, will be your exit.

2. For subsequent rides, alternate your exit between the two jumps.

3. Occasionally, ride directly through the middle, between the jumps.

Doublecheck

▶ Can I control my **focus**?

Focus is the key to finding a direct and natural line from center to center of each jump. Your horse travels in the direction of your gaze, as you also slightly turn your level shoulders toward the final jump. The time to ask your horse for the new direction is just as he is pushing off for the cross bar following the trot grid.

Problem solving

▶ I'm pulling on the leading rein or using a restricting indirect rein to change direction.

▶ I'm leaning or throwing my upper body to the side.

These actions will cause your horse to resist or become nervous and rushed. You want him to become sensitive to subtle indications of the direction you wish him to take.

Learning to use your **focus** even while your horse is jumping is a very important part of riding well over jumps. This exercise is a simple and valuable first step in making focus a natural and effective part of your riding.

Reminders

▶ The single most important aspect of directing your horse is to be clear in your mind exactly where you want him to go.

▶ As you trot into the exercise, think which direction you will take to the second jump. Use your eyes to take you there.

▶ While your take-off for the initial jump should be exactly centered, your landing should be slightly off the center line so your horse's nose is directed to the middle of whichever obstacle you are jumping next (or the gap between them, if you are going straight).

Am I ready for the next step?

▶ Can I ride this line in either direction just as easily as the same gymnastic set on a straight line?

▶ Can I vary the pattern at will, including proceeding in a straight line between the two jumps?

You must be just as clear directing your horse between the jumps as over them.

SETUP

Start with the basic setup from
Exercise 29. Add two more sets of
standards off of the center line, as
in the previous exercise. Build these
as verticals. Use the one-stride
distance that fits your horse.

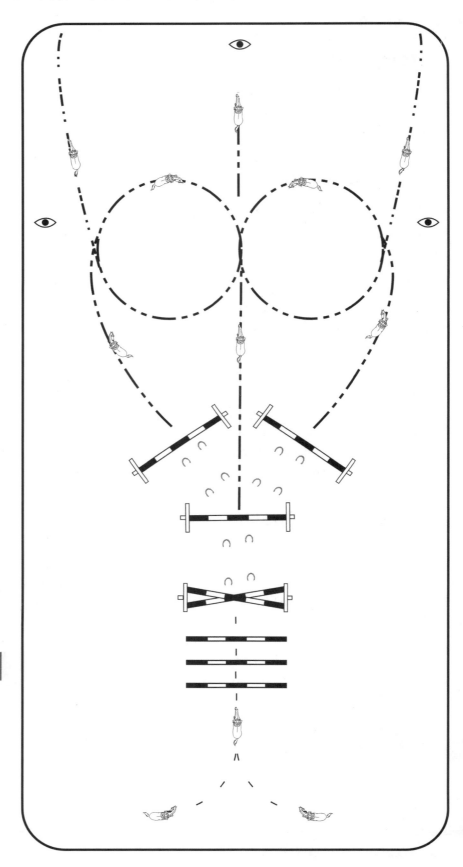

Key

Trot	— — — — —
Medium canter	—— – —— –
Trot-pole	▮▭▮▭▮
Cross bar	◁▶◀▷
Vertical	▯——▯
One canter stride	∩ ∩ ∩ ∩

Two Fence Gymnastic in a "Y"

How do I ride this?

Trot in, as in the previous exercise, alternating between the right and left jumps. Again, your eye is your most important aid.

Problem solving

▶ My horse gets quick in anticipation of the turn.

It is always harder to make any adjustment after your horse has a bit of momentum going. Thus, it is especially important that you learn to remain very quiet and patient through the first part of the gymnastic.

Be sure you are not bothering your horse by pulling on his mouth or throwing your upper body to the side.

AM I READY FOR THE NEXT STEP?

- Can I ride this line to either direction just as easily as I can ride the same gymnastic set on a straight line?
- Is my horse calmly going toward the jump over which I am focusing - left, right, or center?
- Can I vary the pattern at will?

You should begin to feel as though your horse travels naturally in the direction in which you are riding. Very subtle, invisible aids are the goal.

Remember, you must direct your horse just as clearly between the jumps as over them.

SETUP

Set the pattern shown in the diagram, using the small jumps at the distances that require your horse to maintain a shortened stride through the line.

JUMPING FROM EITHER DIRECTION

So far, every gymnastic we have set up has been approachable in a single direction. For more advanced horses and riders (those able do an entire line without requiring longer distances toward the end of the line), it is possible to set some variations that can be jumped from either end.

If you set ground poles at each end of the line, keep in mind that it is possible that your horse will land farther out after the final jump in the line. To ensure that your horse does not land on a pole that could roll, replace the ground poles with flat planks. On the entrance to the gymnastic, your horse will treat the plank the same way as a pole, but if he should land on the plank, it won't hurt him because the plank won't move.

Key

Medium trot   —   —   —   —   —

One canter stride

Medium canter   —— —— —— ——

Trot-pole

Vertical

Oxer

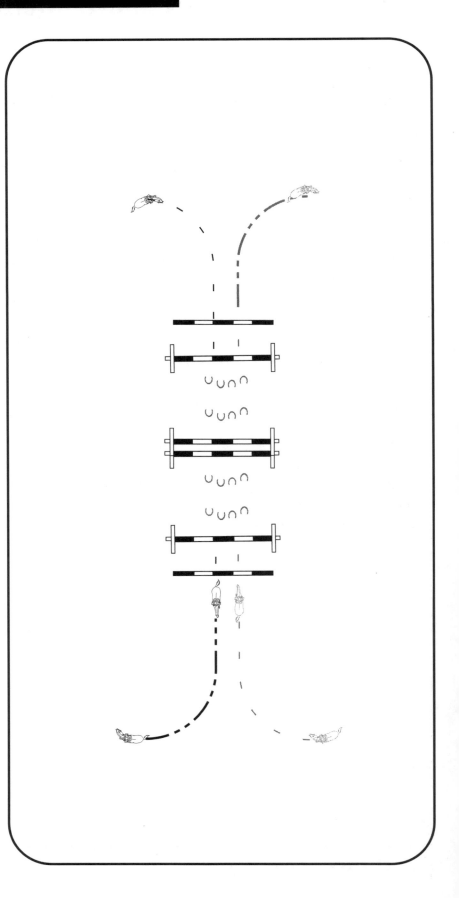

BUILDING A TWO-WAY GYMNASTIC

How do I ride this?

Trot in as always. Ride in a quiet manner, and **wait** for your horse to keep his strides even and collected so that he lands inside the final plank on the ground.

Doublecheck

▶ Does my horse change tempo when going one direction versus the other?

This is quite normal. Horses react to things such as the location of the arena gate or even a buddy or two waiting at one end of the line. Even a moderate slope to your arena where the line is set can make a line ride shorter or longer. Your horse will tend to speed up (or be bolder) when going toward the "good" things or if on a mild downhill slope and to hang back somewhat when going the other way.

Notice these things. Learn how to anticipate and counteract these tendencies. Your jumping results on course will improve.

Benefits

Because this exercise is exactly the same from both directions, it helps you recognize the factors in and outside the arena that affect your horse's jumping.

WAITING

The concept of waiting for your horse to jump is one of the most difficult to grasp and perfect. It feels logical to lean forward to "help" your horse over the fence, when in reality, that action changes your horse's balance and changes it at precisely the wrong time. Tipping forward too far or too soon will make the jump more difficult. Wait for your horse to jump, then keep your body in balance by letting the rise in his body close your hip angle. He will put you in the correct jumping position.

Rodrigo Pessoa on Gandini Lianos.

USING GYMNASTICS FOR BOTH TURNS AND STRAIGHTNESS

Jumping courses consist of jumps connected by turns and straight lines. Riding straight, balanced lines with effortless flying lead changes is an integral part of winning hunter and equitation rounds, and aids greatly in producing successful show jumping performances. However, your horse's ability to land over a fence both straight *and* on the proper lead for an upcoming turn is a necessary, yet often ignored skill.

Landing on the desired lead is the basis for making correct turns over a jump in timed competitions. It is critical that you leave your horse free to jump in an unrestricted manner and use your eyes and shoulders as the means of indicating the intended change in direction to your horse. The photo of World Champion Show Jumping rider Rodrigo Pessoa, above, is a perfect example. He is clear in exactly where he is going next, while permitting Lianos the opportunity to focus on his task of jumping straight out of this combination without a jumping fault. Notice the slight shift in Rodrigo's weight into his left stirrup and the very tight folding of Lianos's left foreleg to miss the pole while preparing to land on his left lead.

The horse's mane obscures the extra release of Rodrigo's right hand, but you can see from the illustration at right how making an effective turn in the air closely resembles the body dynamics of making a turn on a bicycle. Leaning out to the side will result in loss of balance in both situations.

Riding a straight line between obstacles offers its own set of challenges. Again the bicycle analogy is a good one. You go straightest when you "steer" the least. Focusing on a point at the far end of the arena will help you feel both the straight line and the straightness of your horse under you. Any deviations must be dealt with by riding smoothly forward, not by slowing down and making a series of "left-right" corrections with your hands.

As with all the exercises in this book, pay attention to the smallest details. This is how you will become an aware rider with the skills to feel your partnership with your horse and to cope with any situation that might arise.

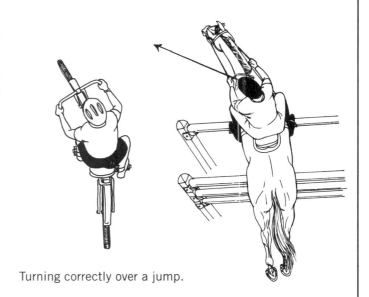

Turning correctly over a jump.

SETUP

▶ Use the same basic setup as Exercise 26. You may substitute a small vertical for the cross rail.

▶ Add two pylons as shown in the diagram, along with one additional ground pole on each side as shown.

Key

Medium trot — — — — — —

Medium canter ▬ ▬▬ ▬ ▬▬

Ground pole ▬▬▬

Vertical ╫▬▬▬╫

Focal point ◉

Pylon O

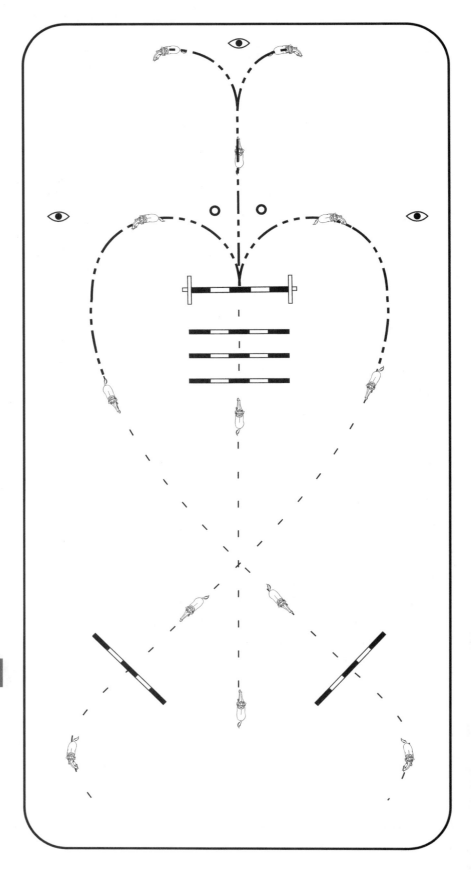

USING THE BASIC GYMNASTIC
Landing on the Correct Lead

How do I ride this?

1. Canter straight through the trot-poles of the gymnastic, landing so that your horse travels between the two pylons in a straight line.

2. Next time through, as your horse prepares to leave the ground over the small jump, concentrate your focus and rotate your shoulders to the left (without lowering your left shoulder), directing your horse to land and turn inside of the left-hand pylon.

3. Continue at the canter around the turn and ride as directly as possible back to the single pole. The purpose of this single ground pole is to serve as your focal point as you come around the turn. Be sure your horse goes over the center of it every time.

4. Repeat two or three times to the left, then work on the turn to the right in the same manner.

5. Depending on the training level of your horse, either:

▶ Make a transition back to the trot before reaching the single pole (in this case place it far enough away to give you enough room to accomplish this);

OR

▶ Canter over the pole, using it as an opportunity for your horse to complete his lead change in case he lands cantering dis-united or on the incorrect lead.

Reminders

Having your horse land on a specific lead after a small jump is something every rider should be able to accomplish.

To avoid interfering with the horse's jumping effort, it is important that you lead with your focus (your eyes), then rotate your shoulders a few degrees, without leaning to the side. This rotation of your shoulders allows your arms and hands to quietly direct your horse into a slight bend, causing him to land naturally on the correct lead for the new direction. Practice this frequently until it is totally natural to both you and your horse.

Begin by repeating the same direction one, two, or three times before changing directions, and be sure also to mix in an occasional straight departure from the jump for variety.

EXERCISE 51

SETUP

Add a vertical fence after the gymnastic used in Exercise 27.

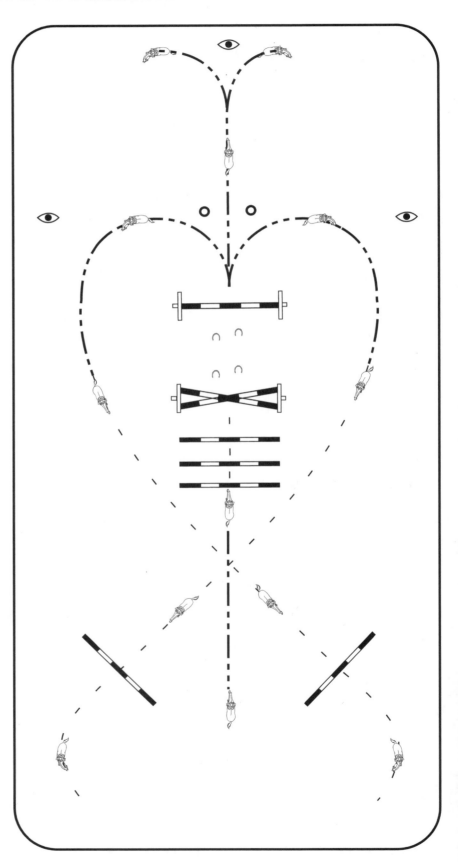

Key

Medium trot	– – – – – –
One canter stride	◡ ◡ ◠ ◠
Medium canter	▬ ▬ ▬ ▬
Focal point	◉
Pylon	○
Trot-pole	▬▭▬
Cross bar	▷◁
Vertical	╟▬▭▬╢

LANDING ON YOUR LEAD AFTER A GYMNASTIC LINE

How do I ride this?

The turn that produces the desired lead remains the same as in the previous exercise. The big difference is that after taking the canter stride and additional jump, your horse now has increased momentum for you to handle.

Doublecheck

▶ Where is my focus? Am I using it correctly?

▶ Am I remaining absolutely straight until my horse gathers himself for the final obstacle?

This is great practice for you to prepare for an upcoming action, while maintaining your smooth and straight ride until the appropriate time to execute your plan smoothly and naturally.

Problem solving

▶ We're landing first, perhaps on the wrong lead, *then* beginning the turn.

Have your helper watch carefully. Perhaps even rake the sand on the landing side of the jump so you can clearly see where your horse is landing. He should be landing well to the side of the center line each time you ask for a turn. If your landing is on center, you are asking for the bend too late and your horse won't feel the need to land on a particular lead (other than his favorite one!).

▶ My horse raises his head as we turn.

You are using far too much hand, and probably using it improperly, pulling instead of leading. Your arms should move in much the same way as if you were riding a bicycle into a turn of the same radius: your right arm moves forward as your left arm comes back, in the case of a left turn.

EXERCISE 52

SETUP

From Exercise 29, measure a straight line, 52 to 57 ft. (16 to 17.5m), and add another small vertical jump. When deciding the distance, keep in mind your horse's stride length; you will want him to land and maintain a quiet canter.

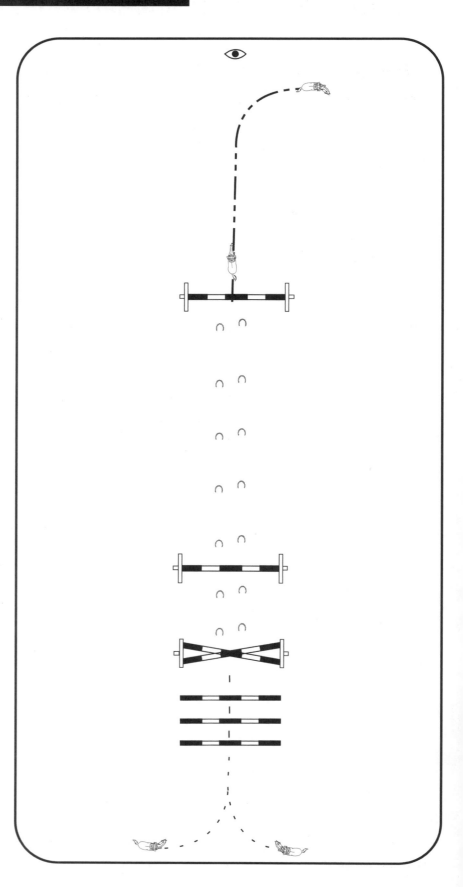

Gymnastic to a Single Fence on a Straight Line

How do I ride this?

Trot in, let the single canter stride set the rhythm, and then permit your horse to maintain that same quiet canter to the final jump.

Doublecheck

▶ How many strides am I taking?
This should be set for a quiet four strides to the new jump. If it is not working, figure out why.

▶ Are the strides smooth and even?

▶ Are we maintaining a straight line between the jumps?
Keep your focus on a point at the end of your arena so that your track is straight as you ride toward that point.

Problem solving

▶ I'm steering to keep my horse straight.
While an experienced horse easily stays straight in a simple line such as this one, a young horse may resemble a wobbly child taking his first venture on a two-wheeler.

Resist the natural impulse to "steer" with your hands. Concentrate on forming a chute with your hands and legs to direct your horse toward your focal point at the end of the arena

RIDING A STRAIGHT LINE

Riding a straight line between obstacles offers its own set of challenges. Again the bicycle analogy is a good one. You go straightest when you "steer" the least. Focusing on a point at the far end of the arena will help you feel both the straight line and the straightness of your horse under you. Any deviations must be dealt with by riding smoothly forward, not by slowing down and making a series of "left-right" corrections with your hands.

SETUP

From the Basic Gymnastic (Exercise 29), position two vertical jumps off the center line as in Exercise 48. Use the same distance to these two jumps that you used in the previous straight line exercise.

A RUN-OUT IS *NOT* THE SAME AS A REFUSAL

It is very important for a rider to distinguish between a refusal and a run-out. A run-out — where your horse evades the jump by going to the side of it — is a steering problem, first and foremost. It can happen at any pace, fast or slow, but becomes far harder to correct when you have too much speed. Always correct the steering problem first.

An effective rider never permits his horse to simply gallop past a jump instead of completing it. Perhaps the best (worst?) example of improperly training a horse is when a rider responds to a run-out by continuing around in a circle in the direction the horse chose to go. Always correct a run-out *immediately* by turning your horse back *toward* the jump.

Reorganize, make another approach, and pay close attention to keeping your horse in the center of the jump.

Key

Medium trot — – – – – –

Medium canter ━━ ━ ━ ━ ━

Focal point 👁

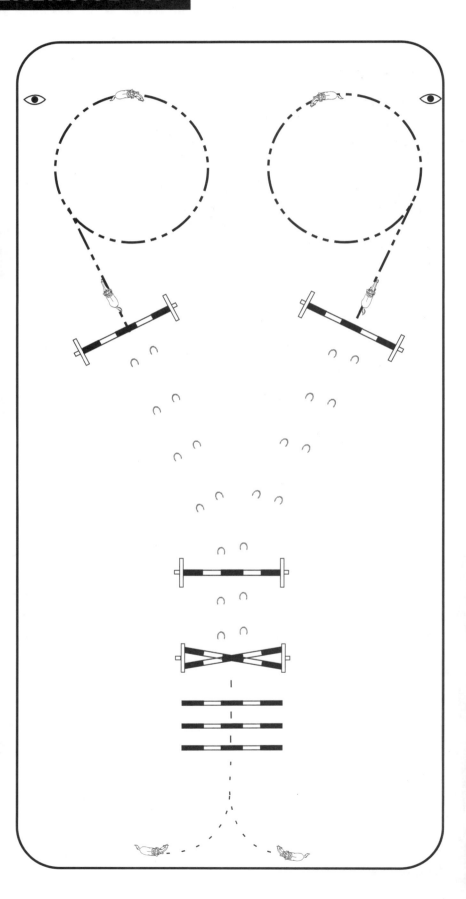

GYMNASTICS TO FENCES OFF A STRAIGHT LINE

How do I ride this?

Although similar to Exercise 48, the increased number of strides between jumps adds difficulty. The additional distance leaves enough time for a less experienced horse to lose his concentration, look off at the scenery, or wander to the final jump. A horse can also begin an almost imperceptible drift that, if missed by the rider, could result in a **run-out.**

Never permit your horse to run-out!

Am I ready for the next step?

Are we comfortable and consistent? If so, we're ready to go on to exercises that include lots of cantering approaches to single fences and lines.

About time, you say, since competitive jumping courses are completed from the canter and gallop, not the trot! You will find out soon how much easier this will be as you use everything you and your horse have learned to this point. With the previous gymnastics, you have been creating some all-important good habits, in terms of both position and focus. Meanwhile, your horse has learned a lot about perfecting his jumping technique and balance.

Before moving on to bigger jumps, return to some of the "poles-on-the-ground" exercises to be sure you have an obedient, balanced, and adjustable horse at the canter as well as the trot.

The majority of top show jumping competitors around the world continue to use these simple ground-pole exercises throughout their horses' careers, finding them useful for attaining the adjustability and rideability that modern show jumping courses demand.

NOTE: No matter what, you must not permit your horse to make the same mistake a second time. In fact, this is a good rule in everything you do with horses!

Hap Hansen on Juniperous at Spruce Meadows.

CANTER EXERCISES: POLES

This group of exercises can and should be practiced with simple poles, first on the ground and later raised up on low blocks. Experienced Show Jumping riders occasionally use cross bars or small verticals in place of simple poles to increase the level of concentration required by their horses.

The work on stride evaluation, adjustment, bending, turning, and collection will pay big dividends in the competition arena, especially for Show Jumping. Many of these exercises are nearly identical to those you began with in Section 1. Doing them at the canter is far more difficult, however, since this is a much more difficult gait for most horses to retain their balance in. The canter's alternating extension and collec-

tion phases require a rider to remain "with" his horse — applying aids subtly and at the correct moment within the stride.

The other change you will notice is the effect of the increased speed. The trot is easy to keep regular and balanced. Increasing your horse's impulsion does little to unsettle your rhythm at the trot. At the canter, however, your horse will have a natural tendency to speed up (and even get playful or strong) the further he goes in an exercise.

Making transitions within the canter takes practice. Working over ground poles is a good place to get it. The time you put in perfecting the upcoming exercises will pay big dividends when you are ready to replace the poles with jumps.

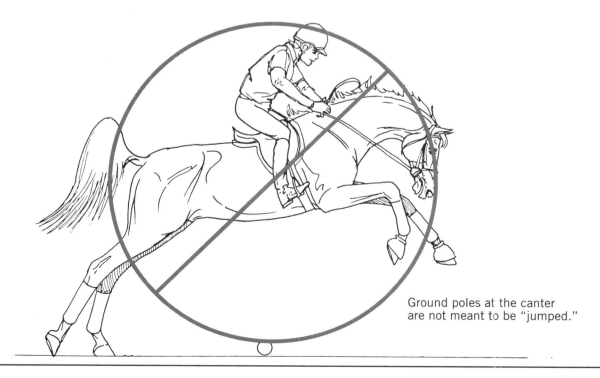

Ground poles at the canter are not meant to be "jumped."

SETUP

Same as Exercise 1. Allow enough room for circles that can range from 40 to 80 ft. (12 to 24m) in diameter in both directions.

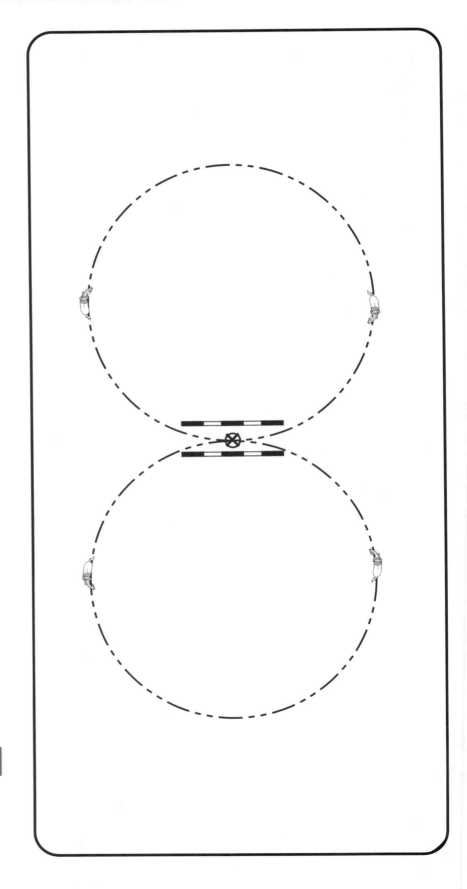

A Chute of Poles

How do I ride this?

1. At the canter, ride the pattern shown just as you did earlier at the walk and trot.

2. Include simple changes of lead within the chute each time you change direction.

3. For more advanced horses and riders, also include halts and flying lead changes in your patterns.

Doublecheck

▶ Can I ride circles of equal size that are completely round?

▶ Can I establish the correct bend in each direction, the shape of my horse following the bend of the circle?

▶ Does my horse willingly execute the change of lead in the center of the chute of poles?

Benefits

This is an excellent way to introduce accurate simple changes of lead to horse and/or to rider.

PERFECTING THE SIMPLE CHANGE OF LEAD

In hunter and hunter seat equitation competition, smooth and accurate flying changes of lead are an important part of a successful round. While changes come easily and naturally to some horses, for others lead changes can present a far more challenging learning curve.

With younger horses, it can be a mistake to make an issue of lead changes too soon. Teach your horse to execute a correct simple change of lead, with two to three walk strides preceding the canter depart onto the new lead. You will reach your goals faster if you take the time to confirm a quiet and relaxed attitude in your horse toward all aspects of jumping before tackling flying changes, especially with a horse that doesn't find them natural at first.

SETUP

Position a ground pole at both ends of your arena. You may place a pair of standards at the end of each ground pole or leave them open as you choose. Leave at least 12 ft. (3.5m) between the pole and the arena railing.

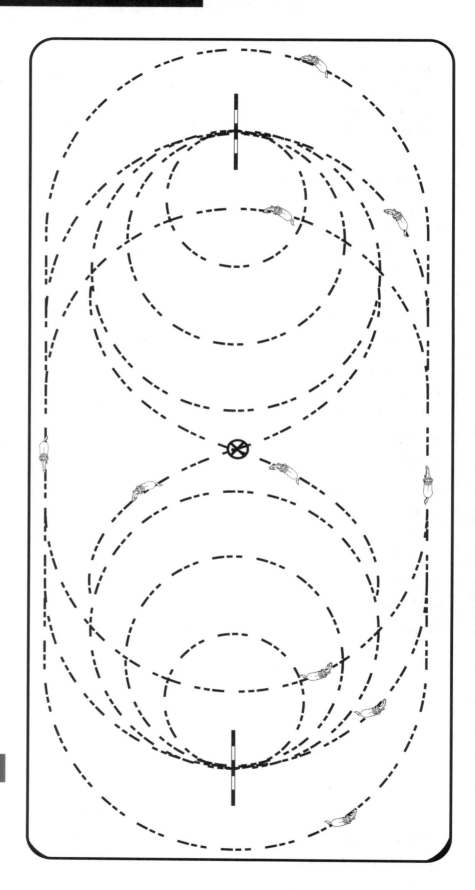

Key

Ground pole	▬▭▬
Medium canter	— — — — —
Simple or flying change of lead	

KEEPING FLATWORK INTERESTING
A Guest Exercise with Anthony D'Ambrosio

Incorporating poles on the ground (and later small jumps) is a far more interesting way to school and condition than doing flatwork alone.

How do I ride this?

1. In your normal flatwork/warm-up, vary how you go around the ends of the arena. Sometimes go to the outside of the ground pole, sometimes to the inside, and sometimes over the middle of it.

2. Incorporate the pole into work on a circle and then a Figure 8.

3. Use simple changes of lead when changing direction, unless your horse is totally confirmed on flying changes.

4. Make your patterns larger at first, then smaller.

5. Avoid pressuring your horse too much. Remember that your horse is ready to proceed to the next step when comfortable with the last one.

6. Work on maintaining a steady rhythm and flow, staying centered and relaxed as you execute the pattern you have chosen.

For the more advanced

Occasionally maintain a counter lead around one half of the Figure 8 pattern.

When you are able to maintain the counter canter to and away from your pole, you have accomplished quite a bit in terms of controlling your horse's direction and balance through effective use of your diagonal aids.

Note

Also check out Anthony's continuation of this exercise in Exercises 85 and 86 of this book.

> *"Doing lots of this work at the canter is beneficial in terms of framing and conditioning the horse, while it encourages feel and timing in the rider."*
> — *Tony D'Ambrosio*

SETUP

Place a single ground pole in the center of your arena as shown.

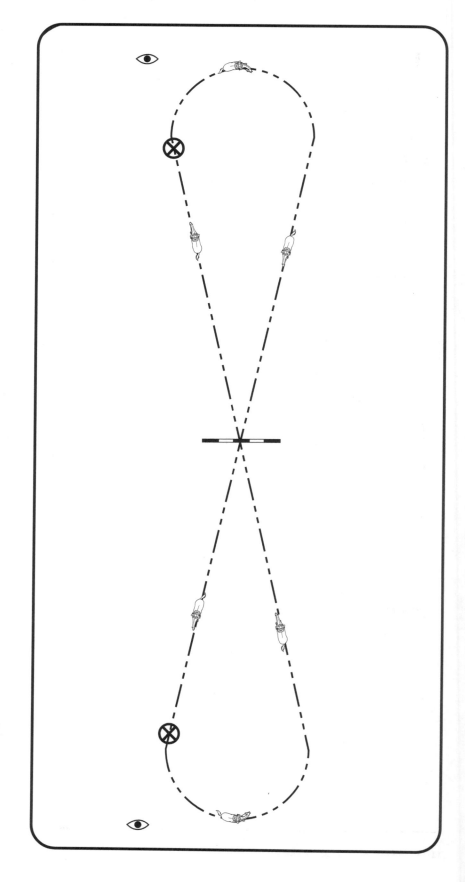

A Long Figure 8 over a Single Pole

How do I ride this?

1. Canter over the pole using diagonal lines that cross the pole at a moderate angle.

2. Plan for simple changes of lead (or flying changes with the experienced horse) at the points indicated on the diagram if necessary.

Doublecheck

▶ Am I maintaining a consistent pace to and from the pole each time?

▶ Can I execute a quiet and accurate simple change whenever needed as I proceed into the half-circle at each end of the arena?

▶ Are my lines truly straight?

▶ Is my pattern symmetrical?

Problem solving

▶ We're wandering toward or away from the pole.
 Cantering long, straight lines over the pole isn't as easy as it sounds. Make good use of focal points. Your simple changes of lead should be both accurate and quiet.

▶ Our pattern is lopsided.
 Be sure your half-circles at the end of each turn are balanced and equal in size and placement at each end of the arena. **Visualize** *and ride the pattern so that both diagonal lines are on equal angles.*

Benefits

This exercise provides practice in going from straight to a bend to straight, while executing straight and calm simple changes of lead whenever required.

Am I ready for the next step?

When you and your horse are comfortable maintaining an accurate pattern, and your position remains quiet and in balance even when your horse makes an adjustment in stride to accommodate the pole, you are ready to move on to multiple poles and small jumps at the canter.

SETUP

Place two poles down the center of your arena as you did for Exercise 5. Allow a distance of approximately 14 to 16 ft (4.20 to 5m) between the poles for canter work.

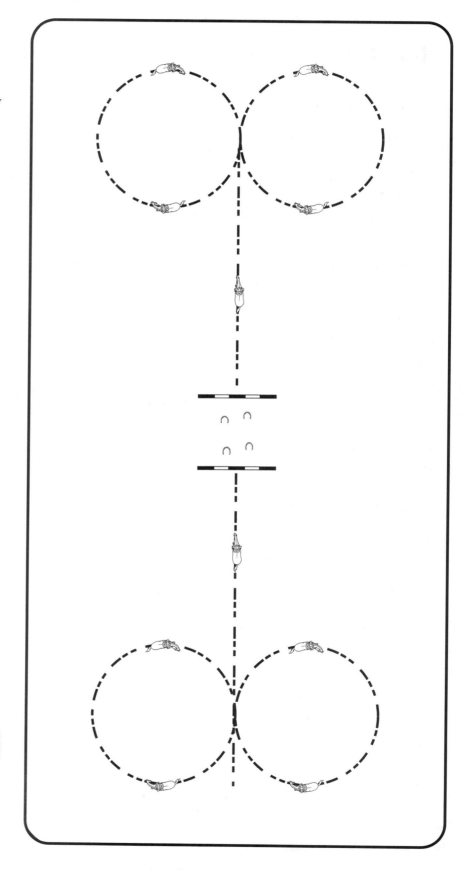

Two Poles in a Straight Line

How do I ride this?

1. Canter over the center of both poles in a relaxed medium pace.

2. Have your assistant adjust the distance between the poles so that all three strides — the stride over the first pole, the stride between the poles, and the stride over the second pole — are identical.

3. Be sure you can ride this from both leads and in both directions.

Hints

Sit quietly in the center of your horse. Keep your eyes up and focus on where you want to go next.

Ride these simple rails on the ground the same way you rode the rails on the ground in the walk and trot: sit lightly and do nothing.

No matter how you meet the first pole, remember, it is your horse's responsibility to adjust his stride as necessary.

Concentrate on the stride between the two poles, keeping it consistent with the stride over the second pole.

Benefits

Your horse should readily canter over poles on the ground, retaining his balance and rhythm as if the poles were not there at all. If this is difficult at first, spend a lot of quiet time letting your horse get comfortable with what to do and how. This will help you practice your waiting skills!

USING GROUND POLES TO ESTABLISH STRIDE LENGTH AT THE CANTER

Ground poles are *not* jumps. You want your horse to take a normal canter stride over each pole. The distances between canter poles on the ground should first be set to accommodate your horse's natural stride length at a relatively slow and relaxed canter.

The distance to accommodate one canter stride between two ground poles is shorter than the distance your horse will require between two actual jumps.

SETUP

Set up two ground poles down the long side of your arena at a distance that accommodates six of your horse's normal canter strides between them. The diagram shows all three of the ways in which you will execute your two ground poles.

NOTE: The spacing that accommodated your horse's stride in the last exercise will allow you to calculate this new distance.

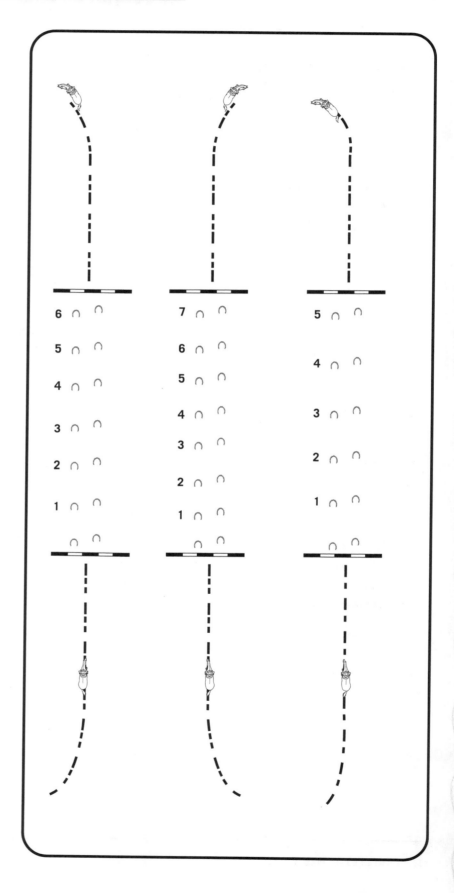

Key

Ground pole

Medium canter

One canter stride

ADJUSTING STRIDE LENGTH OVER TWO POLES

How do I ride this?

1. Canter over both poles two or three times in each direction, keeping your pace even and all the strides equal in length.

2. If necessary, have your helper adjust the distance so it works for your horse.

3. Approach the line with your horse on a longer stride than normal. Count your steps and find a stride length that lets your horse fit five strides of equal length between the poles instead of the six you did previously.

4. Do this successfully once each direction before returning to approach the line again at your normal pace for six strides again.

5. Compress your horse's stride on the approach and throughout the line so that your horse fits seven equal strides between the poles.

6. Practice until you can easily alternate between normal, long, and compressed strides.

Doublecheck

▸ Can I feel my horse's stride length?
This is an exercise in "feel" and learning to recognize your horse's length of stride. Maintaining appropriate and consistent stride length is crucial to achieving good performances over any kind of jumping course.

This exercise can be practiced often, with great benefit to horse and rider alike. As your horse becomes stronger and better balanced physically, as well as more attuned to your aids, you will be able to confidently execute as many or few strides as you choose by asking for greater lengthening and collection in your horse's canter.

THE DIFFERENCE BETWEEN SPEED AND STRIDE

Speed translates to the rate at which the horse takes strides (strides per minute). **Stride length** is how much distance is covered in a single stride (feet or meters per stride). Together these two factors determine how much ground you cover and how quickly.

When asked by rider aids to go forward, horses tend either to speed up or to lengthen their stride, according to what feels easiest to them. It is important for both of you to be able to differentiate between the two. Always be very clear to your horse when you want a lengthened or shortened stride rather than simply a change in speed.

SETUP

Set three poles down the long side of your arena, leaving at least 70 ft. (21.3m) between them.

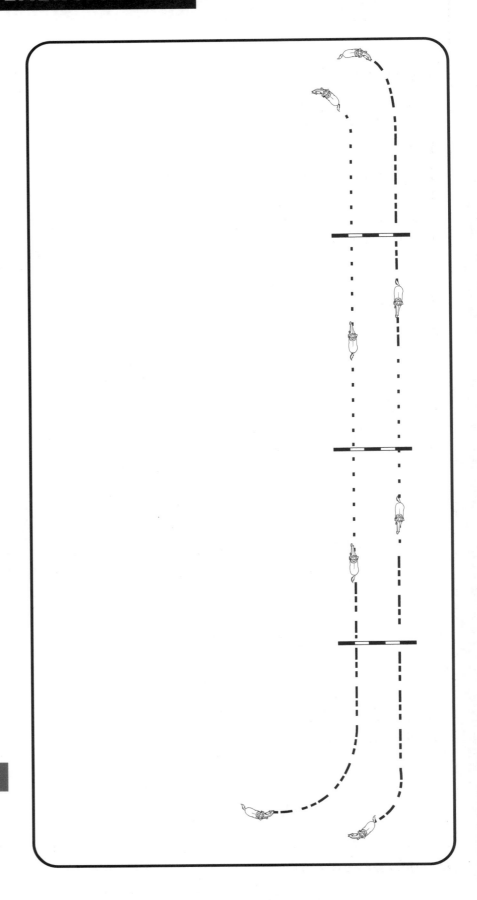

CANTER-TROT TRANSITIONS OVER THREE POLES

How do I ride this?

1. Begin by cantering over the first pole. Come down to the trot for the second two poles.

2. Ride the poles in every possible variation: canter the first, trot the second, canter the third; trot the first, canter the second, and trot the third; canter the first two and trot the third, etc., etc.

Doublecheck

▶ Can I prepare my horse for the upcoming transition(s) so that each is accurate and relaxed?

▶ Are my transitions early enough after each pole to give us both time to establish a rhythmic pace to the next pole?

Problem solving

▶ My horse wants to stay in the same gait through the whole line.

Experienced horses often resist making the transitions called for in this exercise. You must be very clear and definite about what you are asking, especially in the beginning, when your horse may resist. Punishment is not appropriate. Persistence and determination are essential to creating an interested and obedient horse.

Benefits

This is an exercise in obedience. It is especially valuable for a horse that tends to "take over" as he goes down a line of jumps or around a complete course. Repetition and variety develop increased attention to you, the rider.

Novice riders often simply accept their horse's taking control when jumping. This exercise can teach even a timid rider how to quietly yet effectively achieve obedience and cooperation from their horse.

It is well worth the time to master it, and brush-up lessons every so often can be valuable as well.

EXERCISE 60

SETUP

▶ Set a single pole, as you did for Exercise 2, to allow you to make a round Figure 8 with a change in direction over the center of the pole.

▶ Once your pattern is established you can raise the pole onto a pair of blocks.

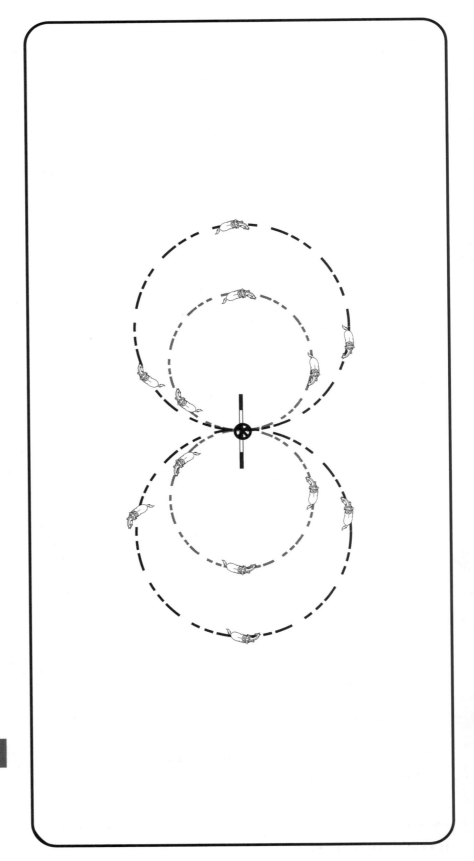

LEAD CHANGES OVER A SINGLE POLE

How do I ride this?

1. Ride the Figure 8 pattern two to ten times at the canter, making your change in direction *while* your horse is initiating the stride that takes him over the pole.

2. Keep your pattern well balanced, with both circles round and identical in size.

Hint

It is important to remain balanced and in the middle of your horse as you change direction over the pole. As tempting as it is for most riders, leaning the upper body into the turn only discourages your horse from changing his lead. Concentrate on changing the bend of your horse's body just as he *begins* the stride that takes him over the pole.

Problem solving

▶ My horse "misses" his lead change.
Stay quiet and simply come back to the walk. Change the lead and try it again. Don't let mistakes frustrate you.

▶ I'm leaning over or throwing my upper body forward.
Go back to the early exercises, make sure your leg is solid, and work on maintaining a balanced and quiet upper body.

Every rider should be able to do this simple exercise perfectly on a schooled horse, smoothly rotating the shoulders while maintaining the correct horizontal plane, and quietly reversing their leg position to change their horse's bend.

On a green horse, it is not as simple as it might appear, however!

CENTERING YOURSELF

It is most important to hold the balance of your upper body over the center of your horse, without leaning.

Benefits

This is one of the most effective ways of introducing flying lead changes to horse and/or rider.

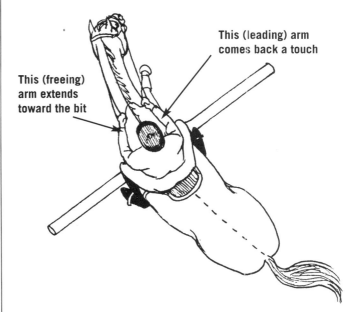

This (leading) arm comes back a touch

This (freeing) arm extends toward the bit

Establishing a new bend to change to the right lead over a pole.

SETUP

▶ Set up two poles with opposite ends of each placed on blocks, with a spacing of 9 to 10 ft. (2.7–3m), depending on your horse's natural stride.

▶ Have your helper ready to add more poles (at identical distances from one another) until you have a line of five or six in total.

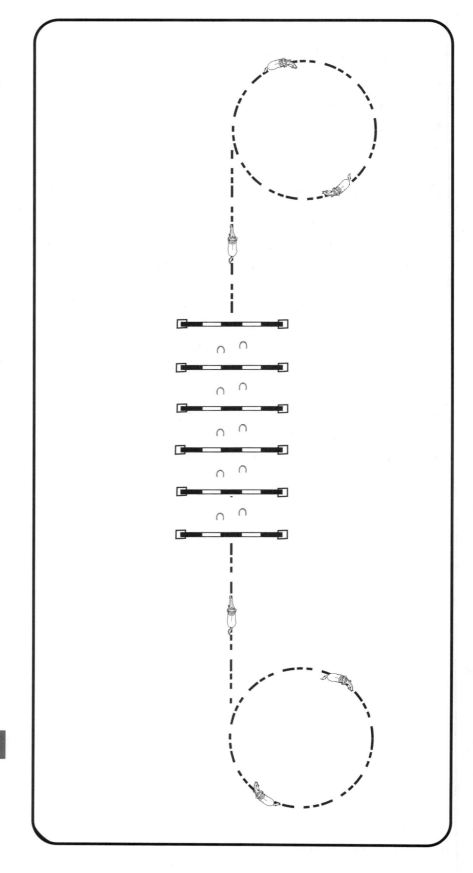

Key

Elevated ground pole ▮▭▭▭▮

Medium canter — — — — — — —

Single canter stride (bounce) ‿‿

LINE OF ELEVATED BOUNCES

How do I ride this?

Canter over the center of the line of poles, allowing your horse to balance himself as he "bounces" over each pole without taking a stride between them.

Problem solving

▶ I'm losing my position.

Time to return to your work on basic position! It is essential that you maintain a balanced, light, and steady position throughout the line. A lower leg that slips backward, a seat that is too heavy in the saddle, or arms that are stiff and unyielding quickly produce a nervous, quick horse.

> *Repeating a line of small bounces, with and without irons, can be an excellent way to strengthen your leg and stabilize your position.*

Benefits

A horse tending to be lazy or one that is reluctant to use his hindquarters can often benefit from repetition of this exercise.

Keep the spacing short enough so that your horse is not **reaching** for the pole as he completes the line. Your horse must quicken his reflexes, continuing to engage the hindquarters well underneath him with each bounce.

For the more advanced

Ride the line with your reins in one hand, the free hand on your head, waist, thigh, or held straight out to the side.

SETUP

Start by placing the poles marked A and C on the diagram.

To create a 66 ft. (20m) circle, which is a good size to work on, make the distance between the ends of the two poles approx. 54 ft. (16m) or see the hint in Exercise 16. As you work through the exercise, have your helper add pole B and then D.

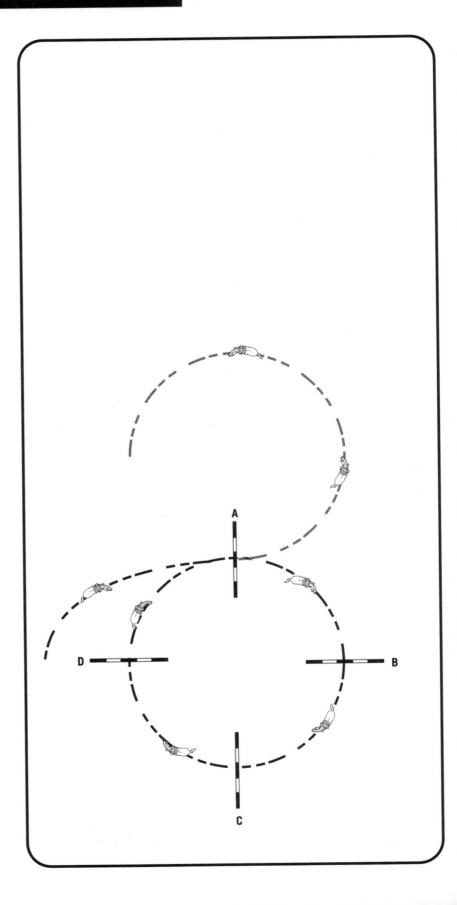

CANTER POLES ON A CIRCLE

How do I ride this?

1. Canter quietly on a circle that takes you over the center each of the poles.

2. Work on keeping your strides and pace even so that your horse takes the same number of strides between each pole. If you find the exercise very difficult, increase the distance between the poles to make a larger circle.

3. Continue in the same direction two to four times before changing direction, following the track shown on the diagram, then repeat in the reverse direction.

Doublecheck

▶ Are my circles round and even?
Notice at which points your horse tends to bulge out or cut in. Every horse does this to some degree.

Anticipate these deviations from the roundness of your circle and counter them with your aids to produce a perfectly symmetrical circle over all four poles. Pay close attention to exactly where your horse is crossing over each pole.

Variations

1. When you are comfortable cantering the circle on both leads, expand your circle slightly by riding over the outer ends of each pole and fit one more stride into each quadrant of the circle.

2. Come back to the center of the poles and your original number of strides.

3. Reduce your circle by crossing over the inner ends of the poles and decrease the number of strides by one if you can. It's essential to be very precise about where your horse is crossing over each pole when attempting this version of the exercise.

4. Reducing the distance between the ends of the poles to work on a 33 ft. (10m) circle requires a great deal of collection and bending from your horse, as well as smoother aids and more exact balance from you. It takes a very well-schooled horse and rider to execute this pattern correctly in all its variations.

Benefits

Perfecting Exercises 62 and 63 produces balanced and accurate riding. It takes a relaxed and effective rider to keep the horse calm yet attentive through all the variations.

SETUP

Set matching circles of poles as shown in the diagram. Use the distance between the ends of the poles that was most comfortable for you in the last exercise.

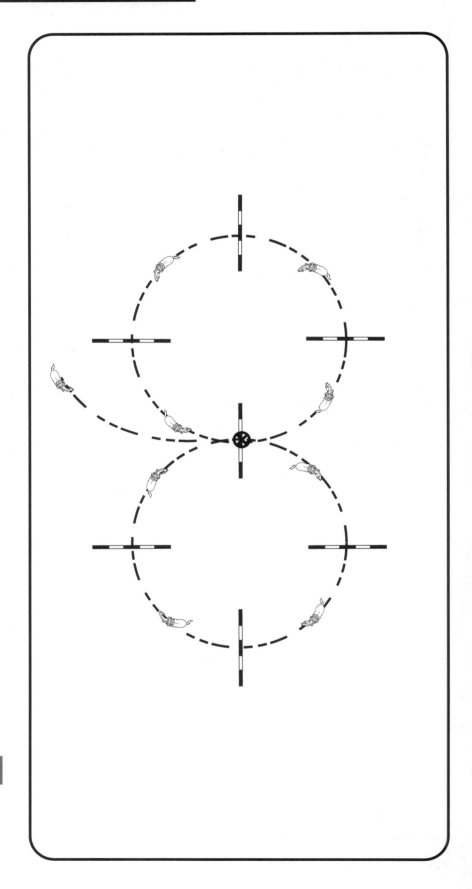

Key

Ground pole ━ ▭ ━

Medium canter ━ ━ ━ ━ ━

Flying change of lead

Adjoining Circles

How do I ride this?

1. Canter one, two, or three circles over one set of four poles.

2. Over the center pole change direction and proceed to complete one, two, or three circles over the other set of poles.

Doublecheck

▶ Am I planning in advance for the change in direction?

▶ Can I keep my horse even and relaxed in both directions?

If you performed an accurate and natural lead change over the center pole (D) when changing direction in the previous exercise, picking up your rhythm for the second half of this Figure 8 pattern will be easier.

HOW MANY QUESTIONS?

This pattern asks several questions of both the horse and the rider. Here are the elements of these questions:

1. executing each pole

2. creating equal arcs in each quadrant

3. changing the bend (and lead) over the middle pole

Counting each individual part as one question, this exercise asks for eighteen specific correct answers from horse and rider.

Don't be surprised if you don't score 100 percent on this pattern the first time you try it. This is a difficult exercise and may take a lot of practice to perfect.

EXERCISE 64

SETUP

Lay out a straight line of four ground poles (set five or six if your arena has enough room). Measure 26 to 28 ft. (8 to 8.6m) between each of them.

Slide the second and fourth (and sixth, if room) poles over to one side so that the ends of these poles line up with the middle of the first and third (and fifth, if you're using six poles). This setup will provide a two-stride distance, center to center, when you cross two poles on a diagonal line.

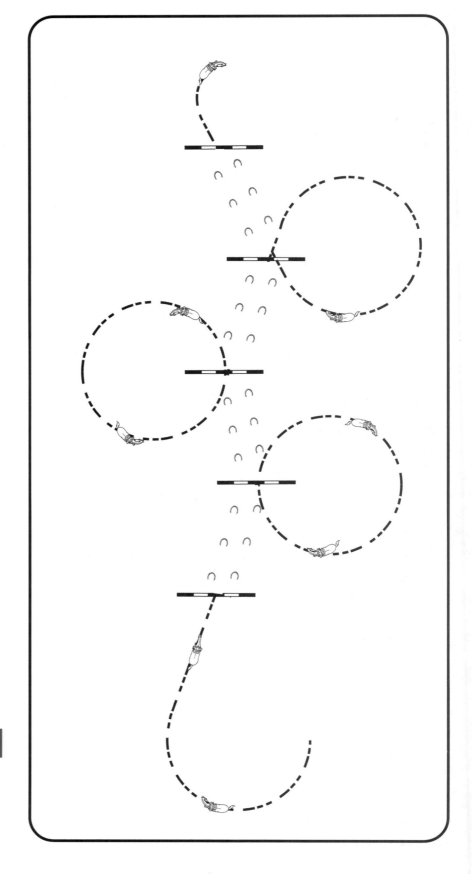

Key

Ground pole ▬▭▬

Medium canter ▬ ▬ ▬ ▬

One canter stride ⌒ ⌒ ⌒

HAP HANSEN'S "CIRCLE-BACK" SERIES

A Guest Exercise with Hap Hansen

How do I ride this?

1. Carefully study the pattern shown on the diagram.

2. Cantering diagonally over poles A and B, continue after B into a circle that turns you away from the line of poles. A correctly sized and shaped circle brings you back in line with poles B and C in your line.

3. Canter the diagonal line over these two poles. After pole C, circle away from the line again before cantering over poles C and D.

4. Continue in this pattern until you have completed all the poles.

Doublecheck

▶ Are my circles symmetrical, equal in size, and located exactly where shown in the diagram?

If your circles slip out of position, you may finish your circle only to find that the wrong pole is in front of you.

As always, cross the poles in an absolutely straight line (no weaving) and in the exact center of each pole.

Benefits

This exercise comes from Show Jumping rider *extraordinaire* Hap Hansen. He has used it with his students for its effectiveness in teaching a rider exactly where they are in relation to the jumps. Your ability to make accurate turns — the kind that you can count on to place you in the precise position to be able to negotiate the upcoming part of the course — is essential to success in jumping or Equitation competition.

And besides, this pattern is fun!

Linda Allen on The Godfather.

CANTER EXERCISES: JUMPS

This set of exercises is especially suitable for introducing a green horse or rider to cantering simple courses in a relaxed and confident manner.

The first two begin through the now familiar trot-in gymnastic, ensuring that your horse will start the pattern with adequate impulsion and a calm and unhurried rhythm. Carrying these qualities into the simple jumps and lines that follow establishes habits that will stand you in good stead as you progress toward competition.

You will notice an emphasis on turns as part of the approach and departure from jumps. With your horse already well versed in making accurate and symmetrical turns due to your earlier work, it is only a matter of applying what he knows to the work over jumps at the canter. Turns and bends as a part of your courses provide an excellent way to ensure that your horse maintains his balance throughout a course. Most horses tend to drop their balance increasingly onto their forehand the longer they canter or gallop in a straight line. The turns remind a horse to rebalance himself naturally.

THE IMPORTANCE OF STARTING AND FINISHING

Each and every exercise, whether schooling at home, in a lesson, or on a course in competition, should have a well-planned and executed "Start" and "Finish."

Your start is usually an opening circle where you establish your horse's pace, impulsion, concentration, and responsiveness to your aids. Having these essentials in place before you face the first obstacle is crucial to good results.

Your "finish" or closing circle is equally important. Never end an exercise or a course without having your horse under full control, relaxed and responsive to your aids. With green or especially fresh horses this might require some effort on your part at first. But it is well worth that extra effort when you see how much difference it will make in your whole performance once it becomes automatic to start and finish properly each and every time.

EXERCISE 65

SETUP

Set up a simple gymnastic. The "one stride to a vertical" used in Exercise 29 is appropriate, although any other gymnastic that you need to practice can also be used. Then add two small single jumps, either cross bars or verticals, as shown in the diagram.

> *The rider's most crucial jobs are to find the right line to the jump and to establish the most appropriate pace.*

Key

Trot - - - - - - - - - - -

One canter stride

Medium canter — — — — — —

Trot-pole ▬▭▬

Cross bar ▷◁

Vertical ▯▬▯

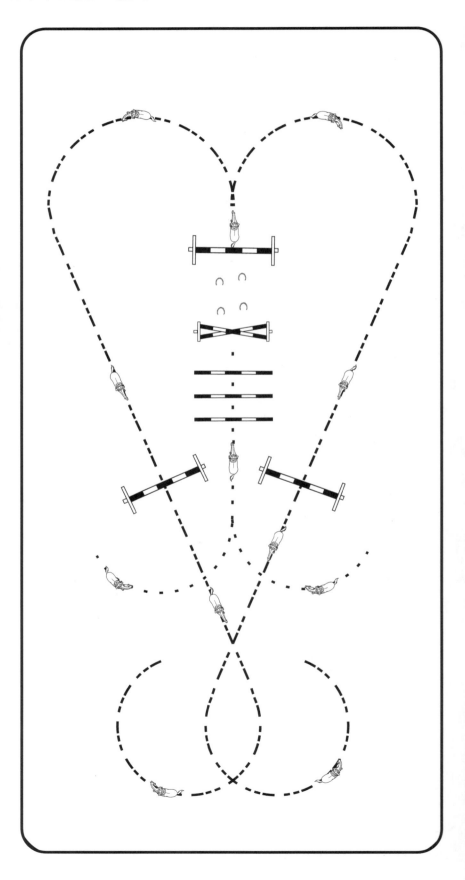

GYMNASTIC BACK TO A SINGLE FENCE

How do I ride this?

1. Trot through your gymnastic.

2. Land on your turn (either direction) as your learned to do in Exercise 52. This puts you on the line to the single jump.

3. Maintain the canter toward, over, and beyond the single jump. Be sure to ride the center of your single jump.

4. Repeat several times, alternating the direction of your turn and the jump that follows.

5. Then change one or both of your single jumps into an oxer.

Doublecheck

▶ Am I focusing?
Try focusing on correctly executing the gymnastic, the turn, and the straight line, leaving the jump up to your horse.

▶ Am I planning a finish to the exercise each and every time?
Plan in advance how you will start and finish the exercise.

Problem solving

▶ My horse wanders to the single jump.
Use the skills you have developed to direct your horse on a straight line toward a focal point beyond the jump. Avoid using strong rein aids.

▶ My horse speeds up when approaching the single jump.
You are most likely getting anxious and leaning forward or clamping your leg on your horse in anticipation of the jump. Focus on repeating the word "Wait" to yourself. Think "Wait . . . wait . . . wait . . ." with each stride your horse takes on the way to the jump.

▶ My horse takes the jump rather awkwardly sometimes.
Don't worry about this right now. Let your horse realize, as he learned to with the poles on the ground, that he must learn how to make the necessary adjustments to his stride and balance to make the jump fit better.

He will learn this skill far quicker and better if you resist the urge to backseat drive at this stage in his training. He needs to put his full attention on his job, and if you lean, pull, or drive, you will only distract him.

The crucial jobs for you, the rider, are to find the right line to the jump and to establish an appropriate pace.

SETUP

Add another small jump after each single jump in Exercise 65. Begin with a four-stride distance. Over these small jumps, this distance should fall between 54 and 58 ft. (16.5 to 17.5m) for most horses. Use your knowledge of your horse's natural stride to decide the precise distance to use for your horse.

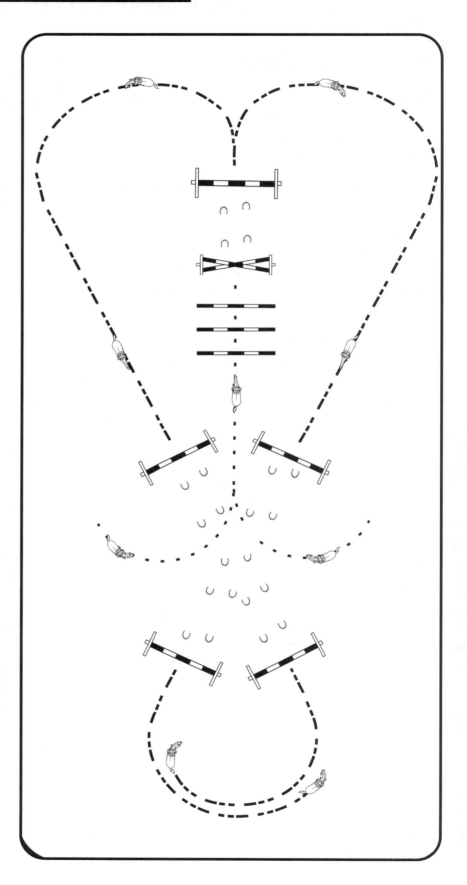

Key

Trot · - · - · - · - · - · - ·

One canter stride ⌒ ⌒ / ⌒ ⌒

Medium canter ——— —— ——— —

Trot-pole ▰▰▰▰▰

Cross bar ⊢⋈⊣

Vertical ⊢▭▭⊣

Gymnastic Back to a Line

How do I ride this?

1. Trot through your gymnastic. Over the final jump, ask your horse to bend toward the turn just enough to ensure that he lands on the proper lead.

2. Maintain the canter over the middle of both jumps of the line.

If the distance you set rides a bit long or short for your rhythmically cantering horse, have your helper shorten or lengthen it a little to assure that it doesn't require your horse to either speed up or slow down between the jumps.

3. Repeat several times, alternating the direction of your turn and the line that follows.

What about Distances?

So far, you will notice that different distances have been suggested in order to achieve the same number of strides under different circumstances. This is because the optimal comfortable distance depends to such a large degree on how you enter the line and what form the obstacles themselves take. Remember ground poles involve no jumping per se. The whole idea is to maintain an even, quiet canter stride throughout the exercise.

Therefore, set distances for simple poles that match just the horse's stride, without any accommodation for take-off and landing. The poles simply provide valuable measuring points. When trotting over the first in a line of two jumps, your horse will not land very far from it and won't achieve his full cantering stride length for at least a stride or two after landing. When approaching from the canter, on the other hand, he will both land a bit farther out and be on his natural stride right from the beginning.

Thus, an appropriate distance will be longer in your canter lines.

In training, it is generally beneficial to work with a little less stride and pace than you will use when competing. Your focus should be balance, cooperation, and technique. Longer distances don't lend themselves as well to this purpose.

In competition, when making eight or more jumping efforts at a pace appropriate to the test, your horse's stride and impulsion will be much greater — and the corresponding distances between jumps are usually longer.

SETUP

Set up this exercise with two sets of trot-poles on the ground and a single small vertical jump halfway between them. Allow at least 80 ft. (24m) between the jump and the trot-poles.

Key

Trot	· · · · · ·
Medium canter	— — — —
Trot-pole	▬▬▬
Vertical	⊢▬▬⊣

ALTERNATING A JUMP TO TROT-POLES TO A JUMP

How do I ride this?

1. Approach the jump alongside one set of trot-poles and canter over it.

2. Bring your horse back to the trot for the poles that follow the jump. Make this transition on the straight line and as promptly and smoothly as possible.

3. Reverse in either direction; pick up the canter again to repeat the pattern in the opposite direction toward the other set of trot-poles, as shown on the diagram.

Hints

▶ Be deliberate in the transitions from canter to trot and strong if necessary, but not rough.

▶ Avoid rushing your horse into the canter after each set of trot-poles.

▶ Work on this until your horse comes back to the trot easily and trots quietly through the poles each time.

▶ A rider who has mastered the skill of the **automatic release** or **following hand** will find it much easier to prepare for and execute this downward transition smoothly.

Benefits

This is an excellent schooling exercise for relaxing a tense horse or for settling one that becomes strong after a jump at the canter. It is also an excellent exercise for practicing your automatic release or following hand.

THE AUTOMATIC RELEASE

The following-hand or automatic release can be used correctly only by a rider who has already achieved a solid leg and secure balance. The rider simply relaxes the arms to follow the horse's motion, accommodating the horse's use of his head and neck throughout the arc of the jump without abandoning contact.

Very skilled riders may even mildly restrain their horse's jumping effort when it could help accomplish an immediate shortening of stride or turn upon landing after a jump.

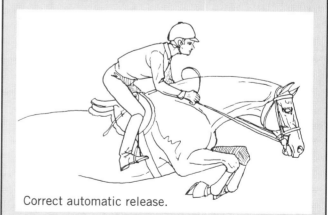

Correct automatic release.

SETUP

Build a zig-zag line of five vertical jumps up the center of your arena as shown in the diagram. Use small to moderate jumps, all the same size, with ground poles placed on both sides.

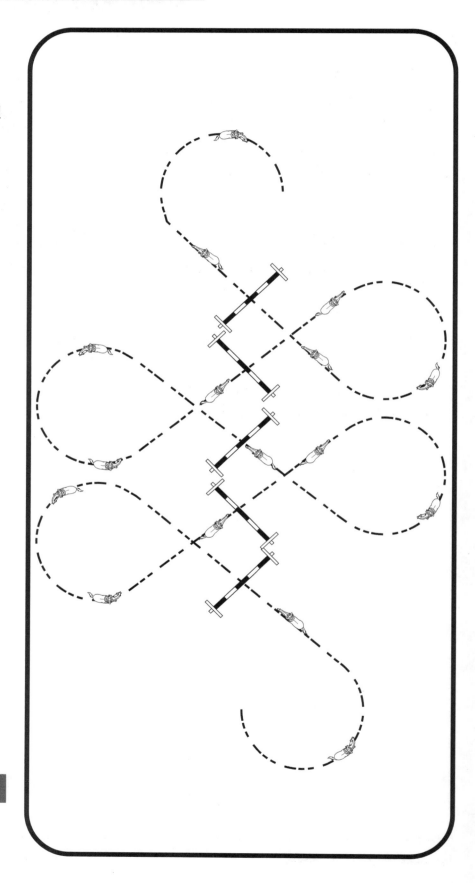

Key

Medium canter — — — — — — —

Vertical

Zig-Zag Line

How do I ride this?

1. Following the pattern indicated in the diagram, canter all the jumps.

2. Make each of the "roll-back" turns symmetrical while you maintain a consistent pace from start to finish.

Doublecheck

▶ Am I planning each roll-back so that I come out of each turn on a straight line perpendicular to each upcoming jump?

▶ Is my horse willing to stay quiet and relaxed over all five jumps?

▶ Can I execute the pattern in the opposite direction just as smoothly?

THE RHYTHM IN THE PATTERN

As you ride exercises such as this one you will find that if you look for the "rhythm in the pattern," it will become much easier. Each portion should flow into the next, with smooth aids, and a focus point that continues to move ahead of your current point in the pattern. It takes practice to achieve this, but when you do you will be amazed at how much easier you will find it to execute even difficult patterns or courses with confidence and polish.

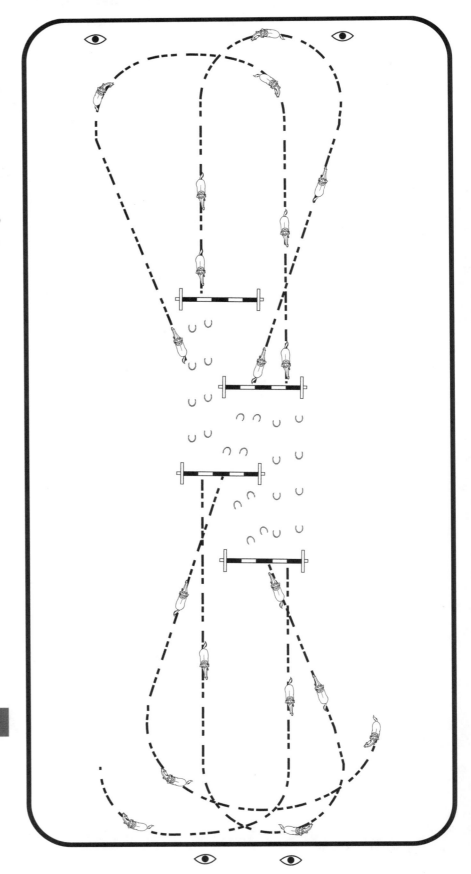

EXERCISE 69

SETUP

▶ Set two in-and-outs. Measure the diagonal between jumps A and B as well as C and D to allow a quiet one-stride distance, and set the direct distance.

▶ Slide fences B and C over about half the length of your poles from the line of A and D, as shown. Keep the jumps small to begin, and place a ground line on each side.

Key

Medium canter — — —

One canter stride

Focal point ◉

Vertical |⊟⊟|

Two Diagonal In-and-Outs

How do I ride this?

1. Follow the pattern shown on the diagram, riding the in-and-outs diagonally center to center.

2. On the lines A to C and B to D, jump the outer part of the two jumps. Make your turns at both ends perfect half-circles. Practice letting your horse do the unrestricted three strides up the straight lines as well as fitting in a more collected four strides when the jumps are small.

Doublecheck

▶ Is my horse perfectly clear about where I want him to go?

▶ Am I going diagonally over the in-and-outs without a hint of a drift?

▶ Are my outside lines straight in both directions?

Benefits

This is a good test of your ability to direct your horse by forming a chute of your hands and legs, using your focal point, and planning your turns so that they put you exactly on the track to the next line.

Executing the more forward three strides in the straight portions will have you focus on leaving your horse on a more open stride on an absolutely straight approach. When putting in a collected four strides, you will be practicing shortening your horse's stride throughout the approach so that all four strides will be equal in length.

SETUP

▸ Place four moderate-sized jumps toward the outside of your arena, centering two on each side. Build each jump with ground lines on both sides so they may be jumped in either direction.

▸ Add a smaller jump (also set to be jumped from both directions) in the center of the arena, parallel to the long sides of the arena.

▸ Finally, place two poles (on the ground or raised on blocks) at either end of the arena in line with your central jump.

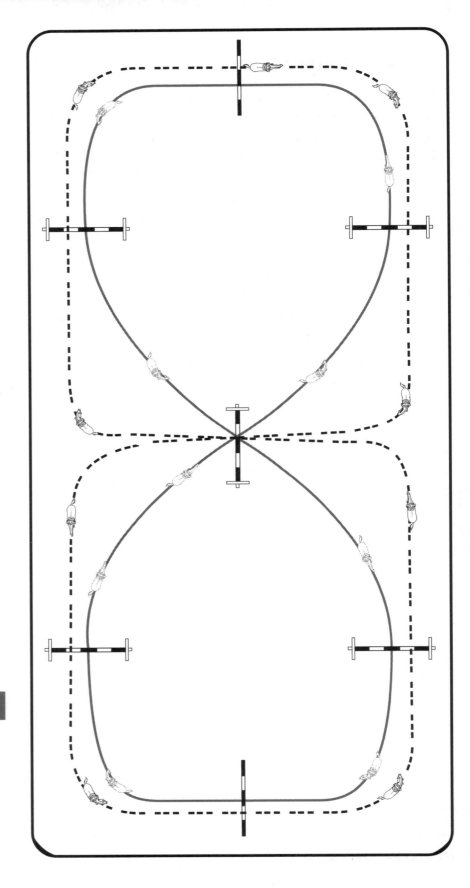

Key

Medium canter (perpendicular approaches)	– – – – – – – – –
Medium canter (angled approaches)	—————————
Ground pole	▰▱▰▱▰
Vertical	⊦▰▱▰⊦

The Jump across the Middle

How do I ride this?

1. Follow the pattern indicated by the dotted line on the diagram. Plan your approach to every obstacle so that your horse is perpendicular to it on the take-off side. This requires maintaining a bend, the shape of a quarter-circle, each time you go from outside jump to center jump to outside jump.

2. Use the poles on the ends of the arena to be sure that you maintain your organization and bend between each diagonal line.

3. When you and your horse are performing this consistently, ride the *same* pattern in a *different* manner.

Follow the track indicated by the solid gray line. Now you line up the center of the jumps so that you approach on an angle and keep your line straight rather than bending between the jumps.

The well-schooled horse and rider will be able to interchange these two types of tracks at will.

Doublecheck

▶ Does my horse prefer the direct approach after I allow him to perform the diagonals in that way?

▶ Can I use my aids effectively to return to the original bending approaches?

EXERCISE 71

SETUP

Set three verticals, with distances between each of approximately 66 ft. (20m). Slide the center jump until it is offset from the other two by approximately half the width of a jump.

Small to moderate-sized jumps are appropriate for this exercise.

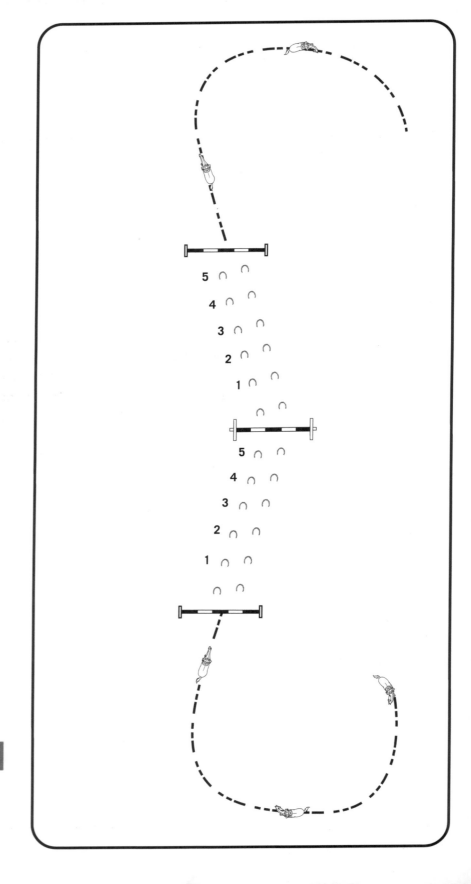

ANGLE-TO-ANGLE BACK

How do I ride this?

1. Canter over all three jumps, center to center to center of each one.

2. At the relatively collected canter that you should use for this exercise, your horse will take five strides in each distance.

3. Do this exercise in both directions.

4. An accurate change in angle over the center jump is required to perform this exercise correctly.

Doublecheck

▶ Can I approach the exercise quietly enough to have my horse accept my request for the change in direction over the middle jump?

▶ Am I smooth enough with my aids to accomplish the change in direction without my horse raising his head or touching the middle jump with his hind legs?

Variations

1. Try this exercise with shorter distances to reduce the number of strides.

2. Also, gradually increase the amount of off-set of the center jump. This will make your jumping angle more acute.

NOT SO SIMPLE

Riding an approach and departure on different angles is not as simple as it sounds. Your horse will naturally want to jump in the direction he is headed on take-off. To change his direction in the air will require the use of smooth and understated aids on your part. Get rough with your hands and your horse's head will shoot up as well as risk a jumping fault with his hind legs. Practice this over very small jumps until you both understand the exercise completely.

SETUP

Set five fences in the X formation shown in the diagram. Keep all the jumps at the same low height.

The middle jump should first be placed in the center of your arena. Place each of the four outer jumps so that they overlap the center jump by approximately one-third the width of the jump. To begin, set a distance of approximately 60 ft. (18.3m) between the outside jumps.

JOE'S REMINDERS

▶ Does your eye create the straight line that will place your horse over the exact center of the three diagonal fences?

▶ Does your horse understand exactly where you want him to go?

▶ Is your horse willing to remain quiet and attentive for the diagonals, while opening his stride for the straight lines?

▶ Are you able to perform the exercise with quiet aids?

▶ Can you do it equally well from either direction (off both leads)?

▶ Are you remembering to start and complete the exercise with attention to every detail?

Key

Medium canter — — —

Vertical

One canter stride

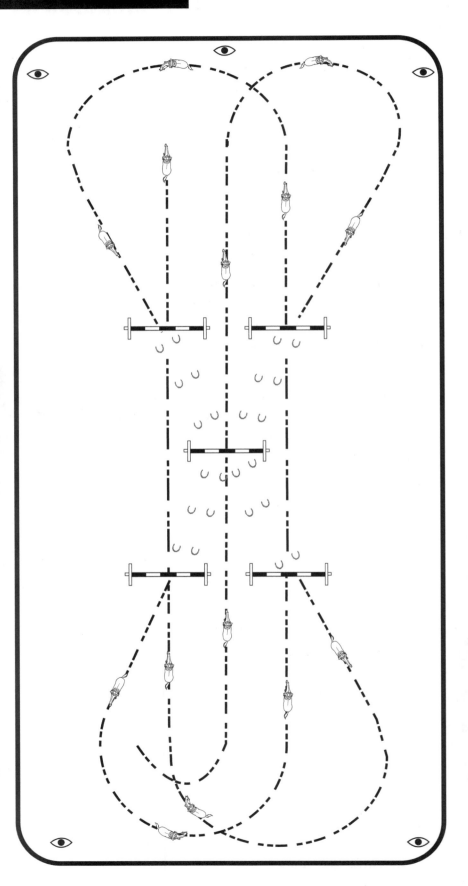

THE JOE FARGIS "X"

How do I ride this?

1. From a quiet canter on a short to medium stride, jump straight over the middle jump.

2. Turn in either direction around the end of the arena to return by jumping across a diagonal line of three jumps — center to center to center. Your horse should take two quiet strides between each jump.

3. Continue around that end of the arena and jump the two outside jumps on a straight line. Open your horse's stride just enough to cover the distance in four strides.

4. Continue around that end of the arena, reestablishing a collected stride with which to jump the upcoming diagonal line of three jumps.

5. Finish by riding up the other long side, again placing four strides between the two jumps.

6. Repeat the pattern starting from the opposite direction over the single center jump.

7. As this becomes easy for you, you can raise the fences and/or further separate your outside jumps (creating more oblique diagonal lines) in order to increase the difficulty.

Problem solving

▶ My horse "wiggles" between the jumps. *Check your use of your eyes. Focus on the straight line that takes you over the exact center of all three diagonal jumps, using a focal point past the final jump of each line. Keep your horse straight under you by forming an effective chute with your hands and legs.*

Benefits

This exercise develops straightness, a quality that is critical to successful competition at any level.

Variations

Alternate between using the longer stride (taking four strides) on the straight lines, and using a more collected stride (to place five strides in the same distance). You can also use this X pattern as the basis for a variety of different exercises and small courses.

EXERCISE 73

SETUP

Set up a course consisting of six different obstacles as shown in the diagram. Each of the six obstacles should be built so that it may be jumped from either direction.

Set the jumps at moderate heights for your horse at his current level of training and experience.

A Simple Course with Multiple Questions

How do I ride this?

Memorize and then ride the complete pattern shown, including all the adjustments in stride length. Repeat the exercise again from start to finish.

Hints

▶ Memorize, visualize, and ride the entire exercise from start to finish. Do not stop or begin again even if you make a mistake.

After you complete the course, let your horse take a break while you review the ride and analyze how it went. Note what went well and what could have been better. Determine where you could make a change in your ride in order to improve your performance the next time.

Again, visualize riding the whole course, this time incorporating everything you learned from your first ride. Only then, ride the course a second time.

Doublecheck

▶ Did I remember to prepare my horse well in advance for every part of the exercise? (This is how you ensure that each portion flows smoothly into the next.)

▶ Was I accurate in my bending going into and out of each corner?

▶ Was I better able to visualize the course after riding it through once?

▶ To what degree was I able to improve our performance on the second ride?

Variations

Try various ways of combining different parts of all the preceding canter exercises to make up new ways to practice what you and your horse have learned.

In the beginning, limit your courses to six to ten total jumping efforts. That will provide anywhere from fifteen to twenty-five different "questions" to answer, depending on how many turns and adjustments to pace and stride you include.

Increase the length of your courses little by little until you can confidently plan and execute a course of fifteen or more jumping efforts. You will then be well prepared to maintain your focus throughout a competition course, no matter what the course designer might throw your way.

Rodrigo Pessoa on Gandini Lianos.

ENCOUNTERING CHALLENGES

This section will help you deal with a variety of common challenges that you might encounter in training your horse over jumps. Each Challenge gives some ideas on common causes of a problem to help you figure out the "Why?". Some review exercises are identified and some new ones are given specifically to address the issue.

It is important, whenever problems arise in your training, to identify exactly what both you and your horse are doing — and why. For example, there are many different ways that a horse might avoid jumping a jump. "Taking the bit" and running past it, going slower and slower until he stops instead of jumps, or spooking right at the jump are just three of them.

> ### For lasting results, fix the cause of the problem

There are also a lot of possible reasons that he chooses to do so. Perhaps he is getting stronger and stronger until control is lost; perhaps he is looking at a new jump so intently that he ignores your leg; or maybe you are just too indecisive about where your horse is supposed to go. An effective rider recognizes exactly what his horse did and has a good idea of why it happened.

The correction must always be appropriate. Using a stick or spurs to reprimand a horse that just ran past a fence is not the right correction; nor is pulling roughly on a horse's mouth after a refusal. Learn to anticipate, compensate, and educate. Remember that effective training consistently addresses the single, primary cause of any problem that might arise.

IMPULSION: WHAT IS IT IN JUMPING?

Impulsion is a measure of the energy and power in a horse's gait. It is independent of speed. The highly collected gaits that are a part of upper-level dressage have lots of impulsion, with little or even nothing in the way of speed. When it comes to jumping, impulsion also involves the horse's *desire* to get to the fence and jump it. Riding over a challenging course of jumps is most successful when the horse has just that little extra urge to "get it done," while allowing his rider to temper this enthusiasm. The result is an ideal balance of aggressive and careful tendencies.

CHALLENGE: RUSHING THE JUMPS

Why?

▶ Horses rush to jumps when they are apprehensive about jumping. Removing the cause of the problem is the only lasting solution.

Hints

▶ Work on getting your horse to listen and relax *after* the jump. This is when you can be proactive without making the problem worse. Having an "argument" in front of the jump could be what caused the problem in the first place.

▶ Correctly finish off every exercise. With enough repetition, your horse will begin to anticipate calm obedience and forget his reason for rushing the approach.

▶ Punishing a horse for rushing — including using a severe bit — is unlikely to work on any long-term basis and usually makes the problem worse in the end. The habit of rushing can persist even when horses are no longer particularly apprehensive.

Regardless, you must form new habits to replace the bad ones.

▶ Fixing a confirmed "rusher" is a long-term project. It is far easier to introduce jumping so that this particular habit is never learned.

▶ Spend a lot of time trotting your horse to small jumps and into the simple gymnastic lines found earlier in this book.

▶ Incorporate trotting and trot exercises in the midst of your training at the canter.

▶ Canter two to four circles after each jumping effort or line; make it a habit to return to the walk only after your horse has relaxed.

▶ Do this *every time*.

CHALLENGE: THE LAZY JUMPER

Why?

A placid horse with a confident and easy-going attitude toward life can easily become a bit lazy in his approach toward jumping — or any other kind of work. It is your job to keep him awake through his lessons, even when he thinks he already knows what he's doing.

▶ Integrate lots of variety in your work. Boredom will cause most horses to doze.

▶ Jump a wide variety of heights and spreads; your horse needs an occasional challenge.

▶ Never settle for a half-hearted response to your forward aids, whether during flat-work or while jumping.

▶ If hitting the poles is the main issue, first be sure that he isn't hitting them as a result of poor technique or an inability to adjust his stride and balance. A good training program that utilizes this entire book of exercises will make a big difference in his jumping style.

Review exercises

Work on multiple transitions over ground poles (see Exercises 58 & 59), putting your emphasis on the "up" transitions.

EXERCISE: JUMPING FROM THE WALK

How do I ride this?

1. Set a small vertical jump and add a ground line.

2. Approach it at a lively walk.

3. Jump the fence without taking any trot or canter steps before the take-off.

GETTING JUMPED LOOSE?

Pinch some mane. Your horse may jump out from under you and you don't want to catch him in the mouth for doing what you ask.

Hints

▶ If he stops instead of jumping, give him a sharp smack with your stick behind your leg and do a couple of prompt upward transitions before approaching the jump again at the walk.

▶ If he jumps the exercise in a lazy, awkward way, use your stick *immediately* on the landing side of the jump to move him directly into an energetic gallop.

▶ Give him a pat as you come quietly back to the walk and try it again.

You'll know he's interested when his walk feels like a tiger, ready to spring off the ground. By the way, horses can easily jump quite large fences from a walk once they learn how.

CHALLENGE: RUN-OUTS

Why?

Choose one:

? Did your horse evade the jump by moving to the side and seem surprised that he was expected to jump over it?

? Did he focus on the jump during the approach, yet veer away rather than jump it?

Same result, different causes. A more definite ride can prevent the first instance; the second requires attention to basic training.

In either case, the solution involves the fundamental issue of steering. You must define exactly where you want your horse to go; use your focus and always fix your own mistake(s) before getting upset with your horse. Determine the proper track and be sure your horse is solidly on it.

If your horse understood where he was supposed to go and simply stopped responding to your aids, it is time to seriously review your basics. Your horse must understand that you are in charge of direction, at all times.

Going past a jump must *never* be permitted.

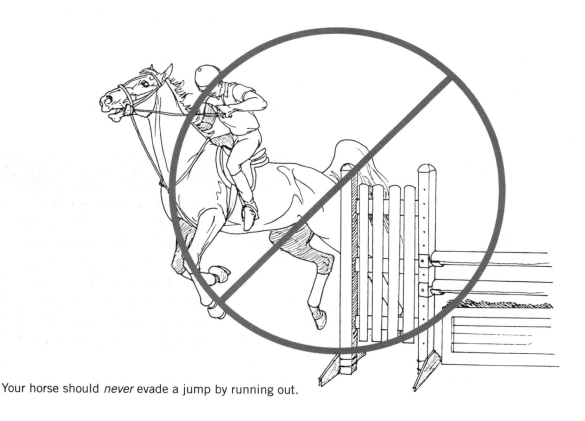

Your horse should *never* evade a jump by running out.

EXERCISE 76: JOE'S NARROW JUMP

Here is an exercise, courtesy of Joe Fargis, that once mastered will leave you confident about planning and riding a precise line to every jump. Your horse will learn that he must go "over the middle."

Setup

Place a single 5 to 6 ft. (1.5 to 1.8m) long section of small wall or simple brush or flower box in the middle of the ring. A short jump pole placed on two or three blocks will work if other material is unavailable.

Start by "framing" this narrow obstacle with a pair of standards.

How do I ride this?

1. Trot quietly over the jump in both directions.

2. Have your ground person gradually remove the "wings" by first moving the standards a short distance away from the obstacle, then taking them away entirely.

3. Repeat the sequence at the canter.

Joe's reminders

▶ Am I keeping my focus ahead, "seeing" the track that will take us right over the middle of the jump?

▶ Does my horse remain calm and jump in good form?

▶ Am I being very deliberate in my approach, using quiet legs and hand aids to form a "chute" to guide my horse?

▶ Have I remembered to "start" and "finish" the exercise, even though it consists of only one jump?

Hint

If your horse is unsure about the idea of such a narrow obstacle, place poles on the ground to create a "chute" on both the approach and landing sides of the jump. A placing pole in front of the jump might also benefit your horse at the start.

Variations

▶ Replace a normal fence with a narrow one in a variety of different exercises, or even create a line of them to confirm the degree of straightness that you can maintain.

▶ Your ability and the level of obedience and trust your horse has achieved are confirmed when a new jump or even a "spooky" narrow fence is no longer intimidating.

ABOUT WALLS

Brush boxes, coops, and walls are now built in two or three pieces (sections) of 4 to 6 feet (1.5–2m) each, making them lighter and easier to move. Placed end to end, the pieces make a normal 10–12-foot-wide (3–4m) obstacle. Individually, these can serve as excellent "narrow" jumps, with or without wings, and can be used in place of wider obstacles in many of our exercises.

CHALLENGE: REFUSALS

Why?

When a horse goes *to* the jump but doesn't *jump* when he arrives, he has refused.

Refusals happen in two different ways:

1. Your horse begins slowing down or hesitating and simply arrives lacking the pace, energy, or desire to jump.

OR

2. Your horse maintains his pace throughout the approach to the jump but "puts on the brakes" when he gets there.

In the first situation, it is essential to get your horse responding promptly and energetically to your forward aids.

▶ Repeat a series of upward transitions on the flat, reinforcing your aids with a stick if necessary.

▶ Ride to your fences with increased impulsion.

▶ If you ride to a focal point at the end of the arena, you will more easily *feel* the beginnings of any hesitation in your horse, which is the point when it is easiest to correct your horse effectively.

In the case of last-minute refusals, figure out exactly what happened. Determine the primary reason for the refusal.

▶ Where were your eyes and your upper body? The simple act of dropping your focus can cause a last-minute shift in your position. For a horse looking for an excuse to refuse, this subtle change in balance is often enough to result in a stop.

▶ Did you have sufficient impulsion on the approach? It is important to develop your feeling for impulsion.

Hints

Riding a horse that has learned to refuse requires that you generate a lot of impulsion without speed. Speed only makes a last-minute duck-out or quick stop more likely.

Be sure your horse doesn't truly feel over-matched by the obstacle. If confidence is lacking, the refusal problem only becomes worse.

If your horse just doesn't believe he *needs* to jump unless it is his idea, it is time to learn to ride with real determination.

Using strong forward aids, contain your horse's pace with firm (but not rigid) hands. Seek a feeling on the approach to the jump that is akin to holding your thumb over the top of a soda bottle and shaking it. Contain this energy until your horse leaves the ground. Release it too soon and there is the opportunity for another refusal.

CHALLENGE: JUMPING TO THE CORNER

Why?

Some horses consistently jump toward the side of the jumps instead of over the middle. Usually, this is a bad habit the horse (or his rider) has developed. It might not seem to matter much now, but when your knee collides with the wing of the jump one day, you will regret not having prevented this habit in the first place! Something that has gone unnoticed until it has become a confirmed habit will always take time and work to overcome.

This affinity for the outer edges of a jump could also be the first subtle signal of a soundness issue. Rule out sensitivity in a front foot or leg, arthritis in a hock, or a stiff muscle in the back or hip before beginning a re-training program.

Pay attention to details.

Review exercises

Review Exercises 62, 63, and 65, paying greater attention to your horse's stiffer side.

While many trainers use guide poles on the take-off side of the jump to work on this issue, it can be more effective to concentrate on the landing.

If your horse lands in the center, he will also take off and jump in the center. A smooth and effective rider can determine where his horse lands with the help of just a few schooling sessions.

EXERCISE: GUIDING POLES ON THE LANDING SIDE

How?

Begin with a single small to moderate-sized vertical jump.

Add two poles on the ground in an open-ended "V" as shown in the diagram. To begin, leave approximately 6 ft., 6 in. (2m) between the ends of the poles. You may reduce this space once your horse is comfortable.

Trot or canter the jump repeatedly until your horse is going over the jump and between the poles in a totally straight line.

If your horse doesn't pay enough attention to the poles, raise them onto blocks to encourage him to avoid them. Use very little hand; you want your horse to correct this old habit by himself.

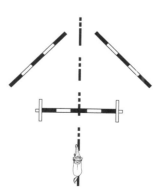

CHALLENGE: WANDERING

Why?

Most young or very green horses find maintaining a straight line difficult at first. When you are faced with this problem, resist the urge to continually correct with your hands. Instead, establish and maintain your focus throughout, including after the final fence of the line, and form a soft, yet unrelenting, chute of your hands and legs.

How?

Set any straight-line exercise (one example is shown in this diagram). Before jumping it, place one or more pairs of poles on the ground parallel to your line. Leave about 10 ft. (3m) between them.

These poles help guide your horse as he learns to negotiate a very straight line between two jumps.

Review exercises

Exercises 57, 65, 66, 69, and 72.

ZIG-ZAGGING

Many horses that have difficulty flowing down a line of jumps in the correct number of strides are actually using up distance by zig-zagging. This leaves them too far from the coming fence, requiring an extra stride.

Have your helper stand ahead of you at the end of the arena to observe the line your horse is following. If there is any sign of wandering, fix this problem first before you lengthen your stride or add more speed.

EXERCISE: SIMPLE GUIDING POLES

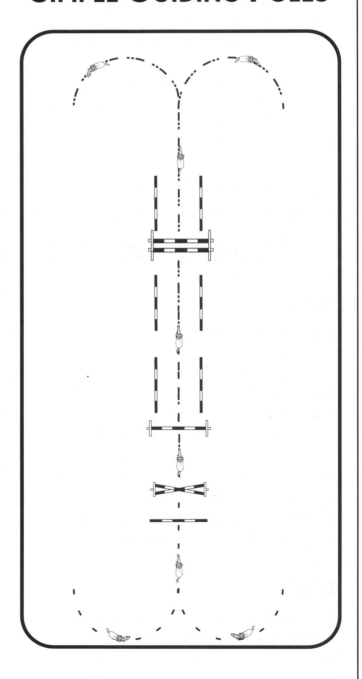

CHALLENGE: LAST-MINUTE EXTRA STRIDES (CHIPS)

Why?

Horses with the habit of **chipping**, adding a choppy, last-minute stride just before take-off, have usually learned this from a rider who anticipates the jump and shifts her own balance forward at the last moment.

Other than permitting a horse the option of a run-out, jumping ahead is the most serious rider error you can make. Horses quickly learn to chip-in in order to regain lost balance just prior to take-off. Many horses eventually learn to refuse.

From your horse's perspective, it is far easier for him to cope when you are behind his motion, rather than even slightly ahead.

Review exercise

Practice the lengthening and shortening exercises over rails on the ground in Exercise 58.

> *From your horse's perspective, it is far easier to cope when you are behind his motion, rather than even slightly ahead.*

EXERCISE: CONFIDENCE WITH A LONGER STRIDE

How?

Use a basic gymnastic such as Exercise 43. Use distances that are completely comfortable for your horse's quiet step. Ride the line in the quiet confident manner you have developed.

As you repeat the line, have your helper *gradually* increase the distance to the final jump, approximately 6 in. (15cm) at a time. Be sure that your horse is extending his relaxed stride to cover the additional ground as the distance grows longer.

Hints

▶ When riding multiple strides between two jumps, the most important place to lengthen your horse's stride is on the first stride after landing. This is when your horse establishes his "go forward" attitude. Never try to make up lost ground immediately in front of the jump.

▶ Have your helper watch closely for any sign that you are getting ahead of your horse in that critical last stride.

▶ When you have established consistency using the gymnastic, place two additional moderate-sized jumps set on a fairly short canter distance. Begin with a distance your horse can handle easily. Then, while you ride back and forth over the two jumps, gradually lengthen the span until your horse has learned how to jump confidently out of the new, longer stride.

CHALLENGE: SPOOKING

Why?

Some horses are naturally more suspicious than others. Some worry about new objects, others shy away from strange or loud sounds. More than a few seem to enjoy playing games with the idea of spooking, even when they aren't truly afraid. If you are dealing with actual fear, even if you can discern no logical reason for it, only patience and the reassurance of consistent, quiet rides will help your horse get over it.

▶ Regardless of cause, *avoid* focusing your own attention (and thus your horse's) on the source of his spook. If the object is outside of the arena or not directly in your path, keep your horse's mind busy and his line of sight directed elsewhere. Work on a

bend that focuses his line of sight away from what worries him. Gradually move your track closer and closer to the object.

▶ If a jump worries him, be sure it is set low enough so he can negotiate it successfully, even if awkwardly at first. He must learn that he can look all he wants, yet he *must* continue to move forward on the track you have set and respond to your leg, seat, and a cluck, if necessary.

▶ Deal with spooky tendencies early on by introducing your horse to a variety of new and innocuous jumps. Always present them first in a location and setting where your horse feels most confident.

> *Teach your horse that "new" doesn't equal "impossible" or "scary."*

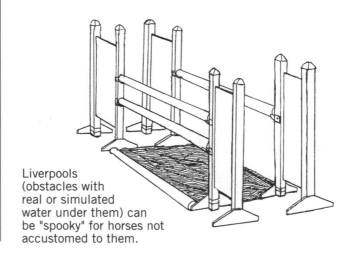

Liverpools (obstacles with real or simulated water under them) can be "spooky" for horses not accustomed to them.

EXERCISE: CREATING A SPOOKY JUMP

Setup

Set a single ground pole in front of a small vertical jump. Lay a blanket or small plastic tarp over the vertical as shown. If useful, prior to adding the tarp, place guide poles on each side of the jump as indicated and allow your horse to jump it with these new additions once or twice.

How do I ride this?

1. Trot to the jump in a calm, confident, yet determined manner.

2. Keep the jump small if there is any chance your horse might jump it awkwardly. You don't want contact with the jump to reinforce any initial suspicion.

3. When your horse is confident at the trot, jump the fence from the canter.

Also shown are two other ways to position the tarp. Placement on the ground beneath the jump serves as a good introduction to **liverpools** (water ditches with rails over them).

Once you have mastered these variations, feel free to add the tarp to any jump in any of the exercises we have already explored.

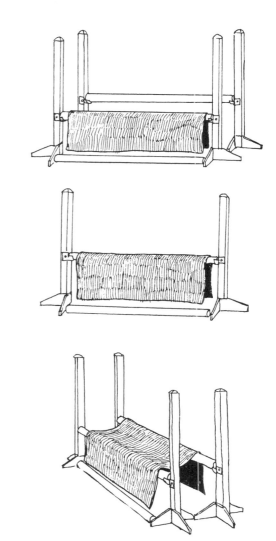

Variations for use of a tarp.

CHALLENGE: DIFFICULTY WITH TURNING

Why?

▶ Failure to provide your horse with clear direction (or giving aids at a time when it is difficult for your horse to comply); *or*

▶ Insufficient training on the flat, with the result that your horse stiffens in resistance to your hand and/or leg aids.

Prompt and accurate turns, so important on jumping courses, are the product of organized and deliberate riding and training.

1. Plan precisely. From the beginning to the end of every exercise, know where and when you are going.

2. Focus consistently. Keep your eyes directed well ahead of you.

3. Communicate effectively. Prepare your horse in advance for every turn.

Review exercises
Exercises 62 and 63.

EXERCISE 82: HAP HANSEN'S CIRCLE-BACK EXERCISE
Advanced Version

Setup

Using the setup from Exercise 64, replace the ground poles with cross bars or small vertical jumps.

How do I ride this?

1. Review the instructions given for Exercise 64.

2. Don't worry too much about the jumps. Concentrate instead on planning and executing your turns in precisely the right location.

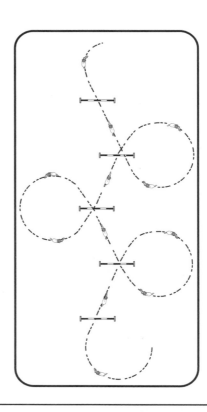

EXERCISE 83: JUMPS ON A CIRCLE

Setup

Modify the setup in Exercise 62, using small jumps in place of ground poles.

   If the diameter of your circle needs to be larger when you begin, this is fine. Just keep your circle round. With practice you will be able to reduce the size of your circle.

How do I ride this?

1. Ride a circle at the canter over all the small jumps. Make frequent changes in direction.

2. Maintain your rhythm and produce a smooth arc in each quadrant of the circle.

3. The turn-in-reverse shown in the diagram can be done over any of the four poles.

4. Aim for a maximum of twelve to eighteen successive jumping efforts before you stop to let your horse catch his breath.

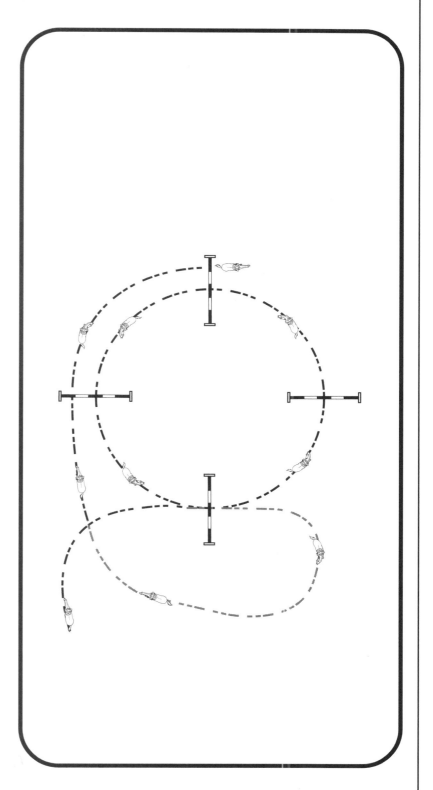

Key

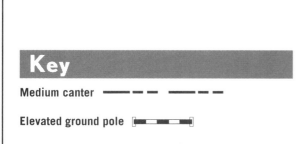

Medium canter ― ― ―

Elevated ground pole ▱▰▱▰

CHALLENGE: LOSING TIME ON JUMP-OFF TURNS

Why?

Slow or rough turns are usually the result of failure to initiate the turn until *after* your horse has landed or nearly landed. Once he has landed, the direction for his next stride is already determined. If it is in the wrong direction, valuable strides and seconds will have been lost.

Shortening your track (the most effective way of gaining time on course) requires you to plan in advance, beginning each turn as your horse is leaving the ground.

Review exercises

Every rider can learn how to communicate an upcoming turn to his horse; it just takes practice. Exercises 59, 60, 65, 66, and 70 are good ones to review before trying the following new one.

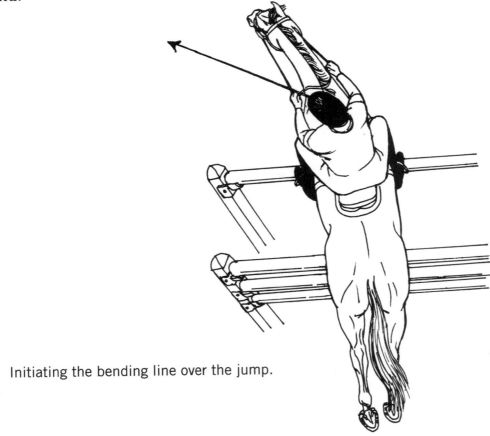

Initiating the bending line over the jump.

EXERCISE: REDUCING STRIDES ON TURNS

How?

1. Set A, a single, moderate-sized vertical in the center of your arena. Add two more small verticals, B and C, as shown in the diagram.

2. Ride a straight canter approach to the vertical jump A, looking for and beginning a turn to the left as your horse leaves the ground.

3. Continue around the turn to ride directly to jump B. Counting how many strides your horse took from the landing of A to the take-off at B.

4. Repeat two or three more times, reducing the number of strides required around the turn by one, two, or even more.

5. Keep your pace *slow* and quiet. Reduce the number of strides by turning earlier and asking your horse for long, unhurried strides. The goal is to have fewer strides on a more direct line.

6. Jump A and turn to C three or four times. Repetition will help your horse learn what you want.

7. Be sure to balance repetitions with enough variety to keep your horse listening to your aids rather than simply expecting to repeat the same thing each and every time. Change the direction of your turn and go straight after Fence A occasionally.

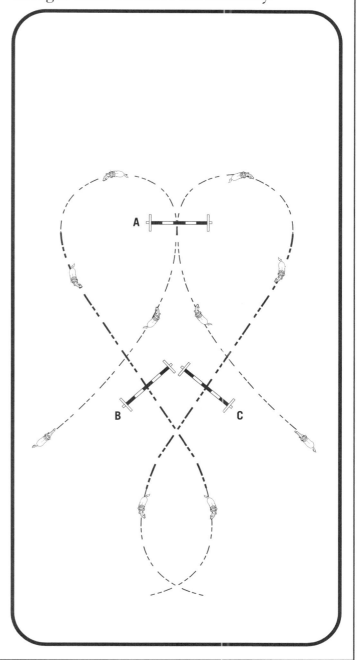

Key

Vertical ┤▬▬▬▬├

Medium canter ▬ ▬ ▬ ▬ ▬

Shortened canter ▬▬ ▬▬ ▬▬

Lengthened canter ▬ ▬ ▬ ▬

Note: Approach the first jump on a medium stride, initiate the turn on a shortened stride, and exit the turn on a lengthened stride. Complete the exercise on a medium canter.

CHALLENGE: INACCURATE CORNERS

Why?

Some experienced horses develop the habit of cutting the corners when going around the ends of the arena. Young horses, on the other hand, often drift or lean to the outside of a turn. Awareness of the problem, like so many other things in riding, is the beginning of the solution.

Anthony D'Ambrosio offers this continuation of Exercise 55 to help you focus on accurate corners. It is a simple yet very effective way to teach both horse and rider to use the ends of the arena more effectively.

EXERCISE 85: TONY'S END JUMPS

Setup

Include a small jump at each end of the arena when working on any course of jumps. Leave at least 12 ft. (3.5m) between the end jump and the arena fence so you can pass it on either side, as well as jump it.

How do I ride this?

1. Every time you go around the end of the arena, make a deliberate choice to go inside, outside, or over the jump.

2. Know where you are going to go before entering the turn. No last-second decisions, please!

3. When jumping the fence at the end, be sure your horse is perpendicular to the jump on take-off, so he jumps it right in the center.

4. To make this exercise more difficult, replace the end jumps with narrow jumps, or even with a single section of flower box or small wall.

EXERCISE 86: REVERSE THE TURN

Another exercise for horses that cut corners on course.

Setup

With a fence on the side of your arena positioned at least 60 to 72 ft. (18.5 to 22m) from the end of the arena, add another jump as shown on the diagram.

You can build the same exercise in all four corners of your arena, or just where your horse tends to anticipate the turn.

How do I ride this?

1. Jump A, landing on a straight line that takes you directly toward the midpoint of the end of your arena.

2. Make a lead change, followed by a perfect half-circle turn-in-reverse as shown.

3. Make a straight approach to B.

4. Alternate this pattern with a normal track around the end of the arena until your horse no longer anticipates the corner.

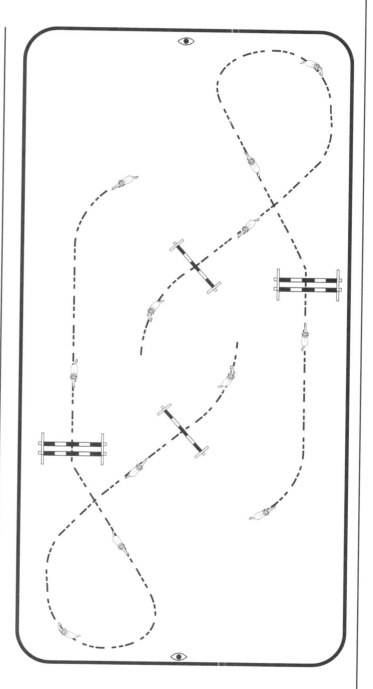

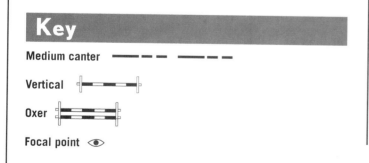

Key

Medium canter	‒ ‒ ‒ ‒ ‒ ‒
Vertical	
Oxer	
Focal point	👁

CHALLENGE: LANDING ON THE INCORRECT LEAD

Why?

If you are out of balance or fail to communicate to your horse early enough to ensure that he lands on the correct lead, it will be entirely up to him to choose his landing leg.

If your horse has developed the habit of always landing on a particular lead, you can change it though practice, provided it is not caused by a physical problem.

A horse's soundness should always be checked whenever he is particularly, or consistently, resistant to landing on one particular lead.

Review exercises

Exercises 50 and 51, along with this new one, are good practice.

EXERCISE: LANDING ON THE CORRECT LEAD TO A SINGLE JUMP

How do I ride this?

1. Ride the pattern indicated by the solid black line. Trot straight toward and over the jump in the center of the arena and land on the direct and forward track to a jump on the arena rail.

2. Practice this approach to each of the four outside jumps.

3. Put the most emphasis on landing on your horse's least favorite lead.

4. When your horse is consistently landing correctly, go on to practice the pattern indicated by the dotted line, maintaining the canter throughout.

5. Continue to focus on being absolutely perpendicular to each jump on take-off, while landing off the center line to assure the correct lead for the upcoming turn.

SETUP

Set up five small jumps in your
arena, as shown in the diagram.

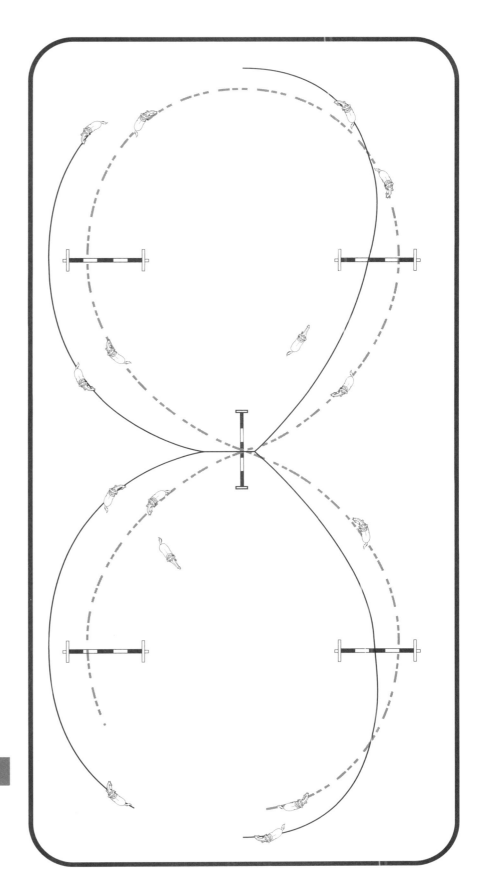

Key

First pattern ————————————

Vertical ⊢━━━━⊣

Second pattern ╌╌╌╌╌╌╌╌╌

CHALLENGE: DIFFICULTIES WITH LEAD CHANGES

Why?

As a rider, you must develop the skills necessary to control both your own position and your horse easily and naturally over the jumps. You must also master maintaining a straight line, an adjustable pace, and an accurate bend throughout. Until you've reached this level of skill, it is best to delay working on flying lead changes in your jumping training.

In the meantime, either execute accurate simple lead changes when needed, or ignore the lead issue entirely. Focus instead on maintaining a regular rhythm and good balance. Even if your horse cross-canters or counter-canters some jumps or turns at this stage, that is far preferable to confusing your horse with a futile clashing of your aids. Without the proper basics in place first, you are far more likely to create an upset or irritated horse than a clean lead change.

Flying lead changes are natural to some horses and difficult for others. It is always a bad idea to confuse your horse. Why should you expect him to be smooth, relaxed, and regular in his rhythm approaching a jump if he is anticipating you galloping, kicking, pulling, and/or leaning after? These sorts of efforts to "make" a horse perform a flying change are usually futile.

Once you have mastered straightness, line, pace, and rhythm after your jumps (if your horse hasn't already begun offering automatic changes on his own when the need arises), use the following exercise to give him the idea of what you want.

EXERCISE: USING A POLE TO SET UP A LEAD CHANGE

How?

1. Set a star of four jumps in the center of your ring. Also place four ground poles near the side of the arena in each corner and a single ground pole at either end, as shown in the diagram.

2. Canter across one of the diagonals of your arena and jump a single obstacle that is in your path.

3. Continue to canter directly toward the center of the rail that lies ahead.

4. Balance your horse's canter as you approach this pole, being sure that he feels totally straight under you and that you are sitting in the center of your horse.

5. Quietly but firmly ask your horse to *bend in the direction of the upcoming turn* as he canters over the pole.

6. If your horse fails to change his lead over that first pole (or cross-canters after it), use the pole placed across the end of the arena as your second opportunity to place him on the correct lead.

7. Finish with a round circle, once again over the end pole, to confirm the lesson.

Rider leaning; horse bent the wrong way.

Key

Medium canter ▬ ▬ ▬ ▬ ▬

Vertical ⊦▬▬▬⊣

Ground Pole ▬▬▬

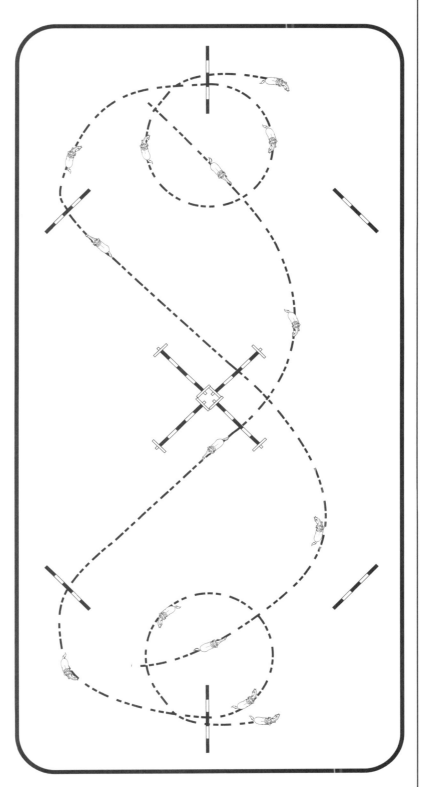

CHALLENGE: GETTING STRONG AROUND A COURSE

Why?

It is natural for your horse to build up a bit of energy and momentum while galloping and jumping a complete course. The trick is to teach him to continue to concentrate both on you and on the jumps, despite his enthusiasm. Every exercise in this book will make this easier to accomplish.

Following are a couple of special exercises to try when your horse is especially strong and fresh or is behaving a bit like a bully.

It makes little difference whether he is rushing and pulling, or locking his neck and jaw as a means of ignoring you after a jump or line.

EXERCISE: REPETITIVE CIRCLES

How?

1. Set a simple line of two fences on the diagonal of your arena. Determine in advance the specific location for a circle approximately 66 ft. (20m) in diameter in the corner of the arena.

2. Canter over the fences.

3. Do *not* stop your horse or come immediately back to the walk after the final fence of the line.

4. As you complete the line, immediately bend your horse onto the circle in the corner of the arena.

5. Continue around the circle, at the canter, completing as many circles as necessary until your horse is willing to be quiet and light in your hand.

6. It might take real determination, along with two or five (or perhaps even fifteen) circles, at first. However, at some point

your horse will figure out that you are going to keep him on this (extremely boring) circle *until* he gives in and listens to your quiet but persistent aids.

7. *Only then* come back to the walk and give him a pat.

Hints

Establishing the inner bend for the circle is critical. It is this bend that prevents your horse from bracing his neck and jaw in resistance. Bending itself will eventually become your cue, reminding your horse that he may not barrel around the ends of the ring whenever he feels so inclined.

Above all, never jerk on your horse's mouth or saw on the reins out of anger and frustration.

Strength of mind (determination and persistence) is a very effective cure for this problem; roughness is not.

CHALLENGE: BUCKING OR PLAYING AFTER THE JUMPS

Why?

▶ Young horses in particular tend to have so much fun jumping that it is impossible for them to refrain from an occasional buck or wiggle afterward.

▶ If your leg and balance are solid (as they should be), this will be an irritation to you rather than a real problem.

▶ Do not punish your horse for playing. It just doesn't work.

When faced with a fractious horse, always ride forward into the same sort of controlling circle described in Exercise 89. Keep your leg a bit in front of you and your shoulders firmly back, in case your horse displays his exuberance with a real buck.

▶ Playing on course only disappears with sufficient experience, maturity, and schooling. In the meantime, give your young or overly fresh horse something else to do that doesn't allow him the opportunity to express his overexuberance.

Recommended exercises

Repetitive circles, even after each line, may be necessary. Refer to the previous challenge, Getting Strong Around a Course (Exercise 89).

You might also add two or three transitions (canter to trot back to canter, for example) or a single circle over a ground pole to your pattern wherever he seems inclined to play instead of concentrate.

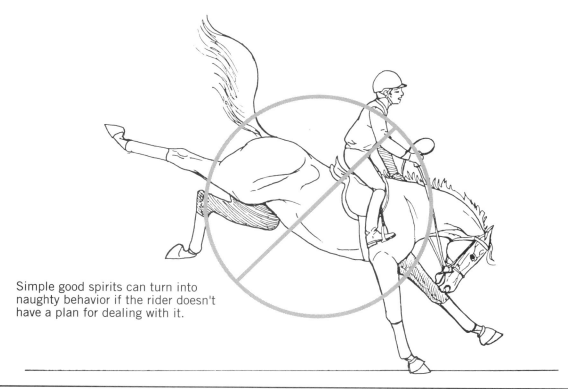

Simple good spirits can turn into naughty behavior if the rider doesn't have a plan for dealing with it.

CHALLENGE: HIGH HEAD CARRIAGE

Why?

Some horses are built to carry their head high; others display high head carriage out of tension or stiffness.

▶ If your horse has this problem on the flat as well as while jumping, take the time to explore the "long and low" work that you can find discussed in any good dressage text.

▶ Be aware that using a standing martingale or draw reins to hold a horse's head down can be a quick fix — but this strategy is never the secret to long-term success.

▶ If your horse is correct on the flat yet jumps with his head too high, the following exercises can be used to encourage him to lower his head and neck over the jumps.

Recommended exercises

Some horses respond to the repetition of elevated trot grids (Exercise 8) by lowering their heads; others get the idea when you set up the following simple exercise.

EXERCISE: SIMPLE BOUNCE

How?

1. Build a small vertical jump. Add a placing pole set for an approach at the trot.

Set another pole, raised up on blocks, on the landing side approximately 9 ft., 6 in. to 11 ft. (2.85 to 3.3m) away from the base of the jump.

2. Trot into the exercise, remembering to establish your pace well in advance and to finish the exercise afterward.

3. As he's jumping, your horse's attention will be drawn down to the small obstacle

he will need to negotiate upon landing, encouraging him to lower his head and neck throughout his arc.

4. Be sure to permit him to do this by giving generously with your hands and arms.

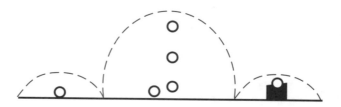

CHALLENGE: OVER-JUMPING

Why?

Some inexperienced horses will over-jump, preferring to launch themselves high into the air rather than risk bumping a pole.

If this is done out of fear or apprehension, you are well advised to take a few steps back and allow your horse to gain confidence over simple exercises and small jumps for a while.

If over-jumping is done with ease and a relaxed attitude, on the other hand, you simply have a horse with more jump than he knows what to do with at the moment. For the prospective show jumper, this is a great "problem" to have!

Your job is to teach him technique, while time contributes experience and maturity.

Review exercises

These horses benefit from frequent low schooling. Spend a lot of time working with ground poles during your flatwork and warm-up. Vary your work, practicing every Exercise from 31 through 54.

Reminders

Be sure your position is secure. Never punish your horse by becoming loose and grabbing onto the reins by mistake.

Should you be riding one of these "high flyers," it is essential to keep your head and eye *up* over the jump. Dropping your head down causes you to roll yourself into a little ball. This crouched position, which places your center of gravity above your horse's back instead of down and around your horse, just might send you flying up in the air should your horse make a big effort over a jump.

Workmanlike position through a bounce.

CHALLENGE: TOO SLOW WITH THE FRONT OR HIND LEGS

Why?

Remember, your horse has four legs to organize at every jump. There are horses that focus so much on their front legs when jumping that they forget to lift their back to keep their hind feet away from the poles. Others have so much hindquarter power or awareness that they occasionally forget to get their front legs out of the way quite quickly enough. Some younger horses have a learning curve until they get their timing straight.

Two exercises can be useful with this challenge.

EXERCISE 93: LINE OF BOUNCES

How?

1. Set up as for the Simple Bounce, Exercise 91, and familiarize your horse with the exercise.

2. Then replace the raised ground pole with another small vertical jump. You will need to lengthen this distance to approximately 11 ft. (3.3m) to accommodate the jumping arcs for two obstacles.

3. As your horse gets comfortable, you will add a third, then a fourth, and even a fifth vertical to the line, all at the same height and distance.

4. Trot quietly into this exercise. Be sure to keep an even and relaxed rhythm, allowing your horse to figure the situation out.

The jumps should remain quite small. There isn't much time for the horse to jump high when executing this kind of line. He must concentrate on synchronizing his front and back legs at each jump, without the opportunity to take a stride between.

More experienced horses can do this line without the use of a placing pole from both the trot and the canter.

EXERCISE 94: LINE OF VERTICALS

This is an excellent exercise for seasoned jumpers in need of a reminder to be quick with their legs when jumping from tighter distances.

How?

1. Set up a line of four, five, or six vertical jumps to canter into. The snug one-stride distance of 20 to 22 ft. (6 to 6.6m) will be appropriate for most horses. Use the shorter distance and low jumps if your horse is unfamiliar with the challenge posed by this particular exercise.

2. Set an exaggerated ground line at each jump, approximately 2 ft. (60cm) in front. (When jumping higher you may bring the ground line out farther, but not more than the height of the jump.) This ground line provides the incentive for the horse to shift his balance back and snap his front legs up more quickly at each jump.

Reminder

It is important that you avoid "helping" your horse with your hands. Keep your hands and body quiet and let your horse learn to take the time necessary to elevate his forehand at each jump.

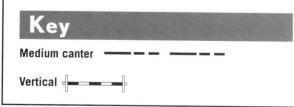

Key

Medium canter — — — — —

Vertical

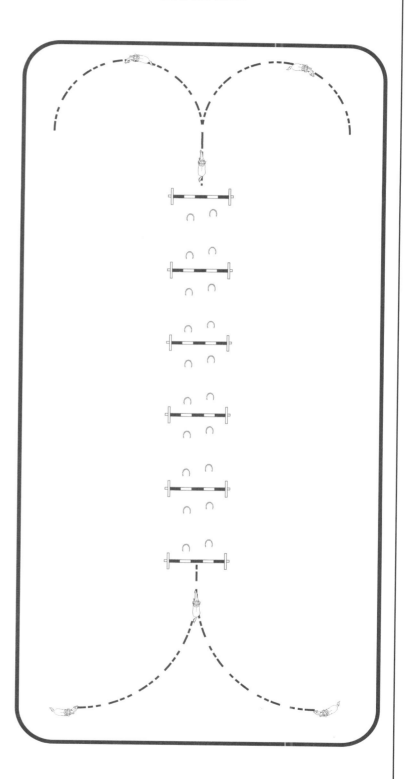

CHALLENGE: SKIMMING OR ARCING PAST THE JUMPS

Why?

If your horse is relying mainly on his quickness with his legs at the jumps, without feeling the need to lift very far off the ground, you need an exercise that requires him to think about his jumping arc.

Here is one that is well suited to a horse with plenty of natural jumping ability that doesn't always jump with a round shape to his **bascule**.

EXERCISE: TROT-POLE TO DOUBLE CROSS BAR TO TROT-POLE

How?

1. Set two cross bars close together to serve as a narrow spread fence, and add a trot-pole a comfortable distance in front of them, as shown. Place another ground pole on the landing side, using the same distance as for the front pole, as shown in the diagram.

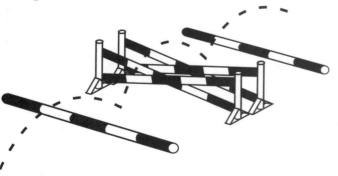

2. Place the raised ends of the cross bars at least 1 ft. (30cm) higher than normal schooling height.

3. Be sure to leave approximately 6 in. (15cm) between the poles at the point they cross. You do not want to hurt or scare him in the process.

How do I ride this?

1. Trot over this spread in both directions.

2. Ensure that your horse's trot has plenty of impulsion, without being fast.

3. When your horse is jumping this exercise comfortably, have your helper gradually increase the spread between the two parts of the oxer. Move each side an *equal* distance out from the center each time (no more than 2 to 4 in. or 5 to 10cm).

4. Gradually raise the ends of the cross bars as well. Do *not* change the position of the trot-poles as you increase the spread.

5. Remember to keep the ends of the cross bars lipped on the edge of the cups as the oxer gets wider.

Hints

In this exercise, your horse will discover that he must pay careful attention, placing the arc of his jump exactly over the center of the jump. He also must take care not to swing his legs, shoulders, or haunches to either side. Your horse will quickly figure out that he must jump higher in order to clear the fence without a rub.

Be sensitive to the amount of effort your horse is exerting as you increase the difficulty. You want your horse to concentrate and try, without being overwhelmed or over-matched.

> *Be sensitive to the amount of effort your horse is exerting as you increase the difficulty. You want your horse to concentrate and try, without being overwhelmed or over-matched.*

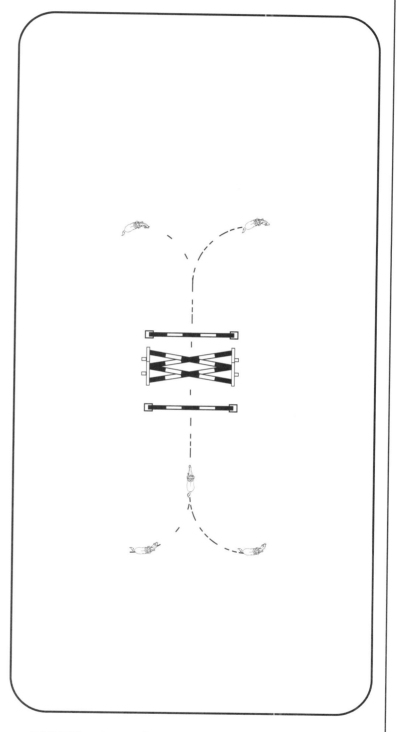

Key

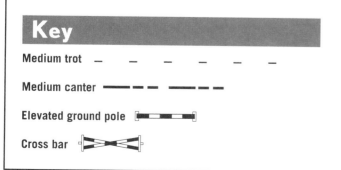

Medium trot	— — — — —
Medium canter	▬ ▬ ▬ ▬ ▬
Elevated ground pole	▣▬▣
Cross bar	▷◁▷◁

NOTE: For safety reasons in this exercise, it is very important that you lip the ends of the back poles on the edge of the jump cups, so that they will fall easily. You want your horse to touch the poles; this is how he is motivated to change what he is doing.

Rodrigo Pessoa on Gandini Bianca D'Amaury.

EXERCISES FOR THE MOST ADVANCED HORSES AND RIDERS

The final six exercises are intended primarily for advanced Show Jumping, Eventing, or Equitation riders. They require a high level of awareness of stride, balance, and impulsion. Skill in communicating, precisely and consistently, what is wanted from the horse is vital to achieving good results.

The first exercise offers a means of introducing permanent obstacles to horse and rider that encourages both confidence and concentration. The others are a sampling of exercises used to fine-tune the performance of both horse and rider — when the objective is excellence in the competition arena.

Jumping Natural Obstacles Correctly

Banks and other types of permanent, natural obstacles are found not only on Cross-country courses but quite frequently in today's Show Jumping and even Equitation courses. Your horse will benefit from a proper introduction to jumping permanent obstacles of all types.

In the following exercises, Olympian and renowned Eventing coach Jim Wofford shares his principles for teaching your horse to negotiate a bank jump confidently and consistently. The same logic and principles can be applied to teach your horse how to handle ditches (dry and water-filled), grobs, and other natural obstacles.

For these exercises, you need access to a small, permanent, preferably square bank, approximately 2 ft. (60cm) tall.

As you tackle these more difficult exercises, the skills learned throughout the most basic earlier work will determine how easily you and your horse will master new ones. When the habits you have established are good ones, they will stand you in good stead throughout your riding career. It is worth the effort. A strong foundation is important — for both you and your horse.

FOR MORE INFORMATION . . .

Jim Wofford's excellent book *Gymnastics: Systematic Training for Jumping Horses* contains many other beautifully explained and illustrated gymnastic exercises that horsemen from any discipline will find valuable.

INTRODUCING A BANK JUMP

How do I ride this?

1. Let your horse familiarize himself with the change in levels by "hopping" up and down the bank from a trot and canter.

Landing at a different level than your take-off requires particular awareness of your balance on your horse. Prior experience jumping small obstacles on sloping ground can be very helpful.

2. When jumping up onto a bank, your weight needs to be securely in your heel. Keep your center of gravity up near your horse's shoulders as he jumps. Approaching the bank with your reins too long will make the proper position far more difficult and may cause your balance to fall behind your horse.

3. When jumping down off of the bank, keep your lower leg on or slightly in front of the girth. Your center of gravity should remain slightly behind your horse's shoulders.

4. Make sure your arms are relaxed at all times and that you can easily allow the reins to slip through your hands in case your horse surprises you with a bigger jump than expected onto or off of the bank.

JIM'S REMINDERS

Jumping down will give you the feeling that you will land very close to the jump at the bottom. Do not panic and pull back on the reins in an attempt to shorten your horse's stride.

"Like so many things in riding this actually creates the condition that you were trying to prevent," Jim says in his book (see appendix). In this case, pulling back causes your horse to invert his back and jump even farther off the bank.

Instead, trot your approach to A and direct your thinking toward having your horse step quietly down off the bank, landing as close to it as possible to gain the maximum amount of room for his stride in front of the jump.

Proper balance jumping off a small bank.

EXERCISE 97: A BANK GYMNASTIC

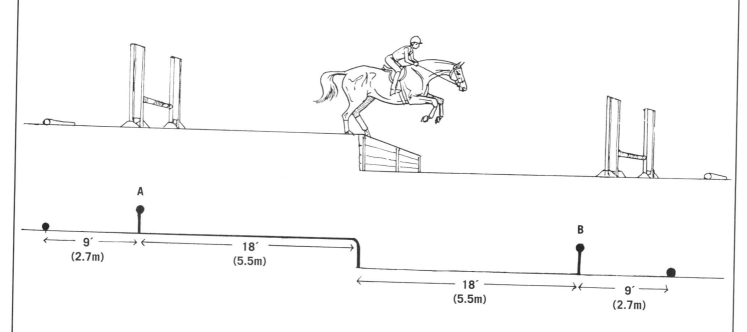

A

9′
(2.7m)

18′
(5.5m)

B

18′
(5.5m)

9′
(2.7m)

To teach your horse how to handle banks smoothly and in rhythm, build up the following exercise in the sequence described below.

Setup

1. Place standards at locations A and B as shown on the diagram above.

2. Start with a pole on the ground between the standards at A, with a placing pole 9 ft. (2.7m) in front of it.

How do I ride this?

1. Jump this in each direction. Approach first at the trot and then at the canter.

2. When your horse is comfortable with this, build a small vertical at A, leaving the placing pole 9 ft. (2.7m) in front.

3. Approach at the trot from the A direction. Your horse will take one canter stride before stepping off the bank and cantering through the still-empty standards at B.

4. Approach from the B direction, riding a canter up onto the bank.

5. When your horse is comfortable with this, you can add another small vertical on the B standards with a placing pole 9 ft. (2.7m) in front as shown.

6. Approach at the canter from B toward the bank so that the new part of the exercise is the first part that your horse sees.

7. Once your horse has jumped successfully — landing over B, taking a stride, jumping up the bank, taking another single stride, jumping again, and landing after A in a poised and balanced fashion — you are ready to come back the other way around.

SIX – SEVEN – SIX – FIVE – SIX

Setup

▶ Set two moderate-sized jumps in a straight line.

▶ Build each fence so it may be jumped in either direction. A distance of 76 ft. (23m) will work well for the average horse.

Hint

The greatest value of this exercise comes when you merely *indicate* what the horse should do. Be willing to let your horse execute the jumps. The less you distract your horse with last-minute adjustments, the greater his opportunity to concentrate on the fence and jump it without a fault.

Very advanced horses and riders can set this exercise at a shorter distance for an option of six, five, or four strides. With fewer steps to work with, the adjustment to stride length has to be greater.

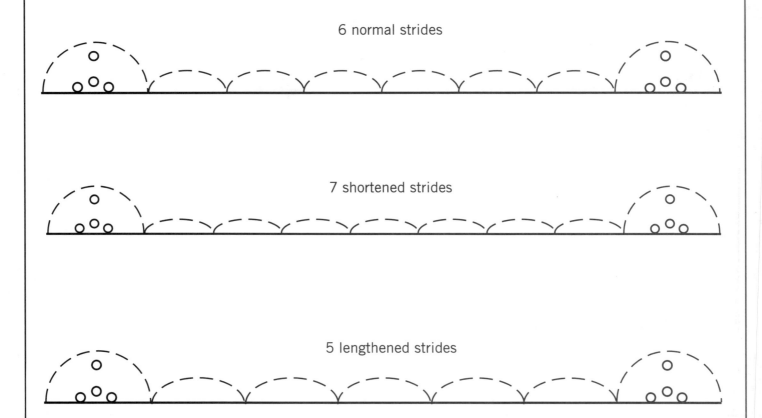

6 normal strides

7 shortened strides

5 lengthened strides

How do I ride this?

1. Canter the line at least once in each direction, approaching at a medium canter. Fit six uniform strides into the line.

2. When your horse is in a comfortable "groove," approach the first jump of the line with reduced impulsion, and ride very quietly off of the ground. In this way, you are asking your horse to land *shallow* (close to the jump). Continue with shorter strides at the beginning of the line to allow your horse to comfortably add another stride between the jumps.

You should not pull on your horse in front of the second jump to fit in the seventh stride. Learn what you need to do to communicate to your horse that he must contain his stride *early* in the line to make the extra stride fit.

Repeat once or twice and then return to entering at your medium pace and placing six strides between the jumps.

3. Next ride the same line asking your horse for five strides between the two jumps.

To achieve this, increase your impulsion slightly on the approach to the first jump, but don't increase your speed and stride. Encourage your horse to leave the ground with greater energy and land farther out from the jump.

Establish a slightly more open stride within the first two strides after landing. Then there will be no need to push your horse in front of the second fence. With practice, good riding, and a well-schooled horse, you should be able to execute this line at will in any of its variations, using only a very small (and nearly invisible) adjustment in impulsion, stride, and balance.

Doublecheck

▶ Does my horse clearly understand what I am asking in this exercise?

▶ Can I establish the appropriate energy and stride length *immediately* upon landing?

▶ Am I able to resist the urge to slow down or speed up on the approach to the first jump?

▶ Can I feel precisely when I have made sufficient adjustment to ensure that my horse takes the desired number of strides? Can I avoid overcorrecting or giving my horse any more assistance than he needs at the second jump?

SETUP

Set four oxers (not too wide) toward the corners of your arena, with a double of verticals centered between them as shown. Use a distance of between 21 and 23 ft. (6.2 up to 7m) for the double, depending on the size of the jumps and your horse's stride length and level of experience.

Measure on the bending line from the double to each of the oxers, setting an *easy* five stride distance to begin (approximately 69 ft., or 21m, for most horses.)

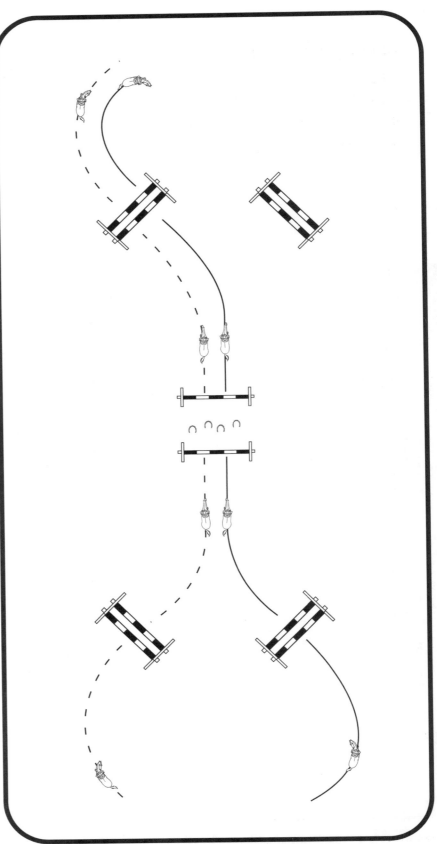

Key

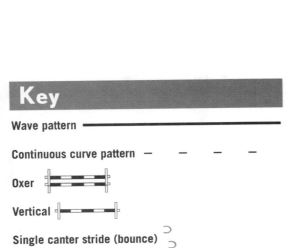

Wave pattern ————————

Continuous curve pattern — — — —

Oxer

Vertical

Single canter stride (bounce)

BENDING TO STRAIGHT TO BENDING

How do I ride this?

1. Ride all varieties of lines shown: the wave pattern (solid line), beginning with each of the four oxers, as well as the continuous curve (dotted line), also beginning from each corner.

2. To increase the difficulty of the exercise, set the oxers to require more bend, or use distances that demand an adjustment in stride (or even a choice in number of strides) on either side of the double.

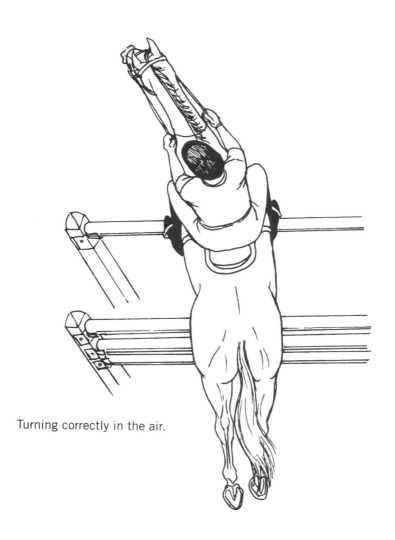

Turning correctly in the air.

SETUP

1. Place five pairs of standards in a straight line where you can approach from both directions and on both leads.

2. Set a distance of 11 to 12 ft. (3.3 to 3.7m) from A to B, and repeat this distance from D to E. The distance from B to C, and again from C to D, should be 21 to 22 ft. (6.4 to 6.7m).

3. Build small to moderate-sized verticals, with ground lines on both sides, on all but the middle set of standards. At the start, leave these standards empty.

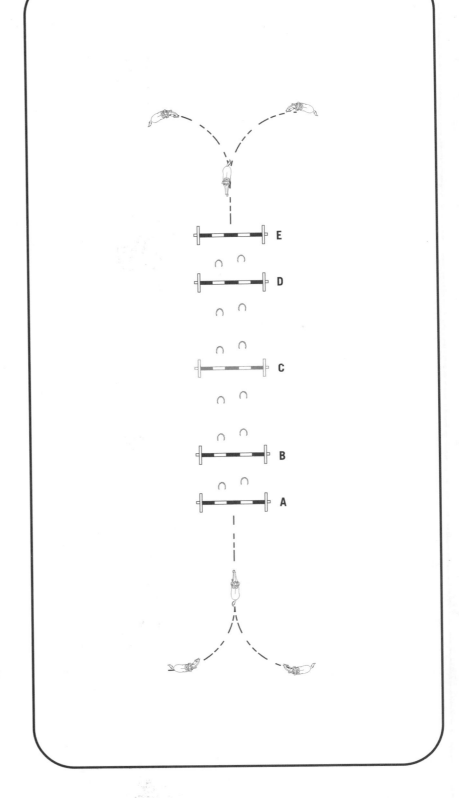

Key

Medium canter — — — — — —

Vertical ⊢━━━━⊣

Single canter stride (bounce)

BOUNCE TO BOUNCE, PLUS A VERTICAL
A Guest Exercise with Anthony D'Ambrosio

Here's another valuable exercise provided by course designer and trainer/rider Anthony D'Ambrosio. This canter gymnastic is far easier to set up than to ride well. It teaches your horse a lot about maintaining his balance in combinations and related lines. It also helps you learn to remain quiet and in perfect balance with your horse.

How do I ride this?

1. Canter back and forth through this exercise at a medium pace. Your horse will bounce the first two elements, and canter three strides before bouncing the final two. Keep your horse in a very straight line throughout, maintaining an even rhythm from one end to the other.

2. When your horse does this equally well from both directions and on both leads, have your helper add the rails to build a moderate jump on your center standards.

Now the sequence will be: bounce, one stride, one stride, bounce, with your horse remaining very balanced and collected throughout.

Variation

To increase your horse's flexibility and concentration after he is confident with the exercise:

1. Have your helper raise the center jump 4 to 9 in. (10 to 20cm) higher than the other four.

2. Jump the line in both directions.

3. Lower the center jump and raise the second and fourth elements.

Unless you and your horse are very experienced with these types of exercises, avoid raising every jump in a multiple line at the same time. This is seldom necessary to get your horse's attention focused on the job at hand. Raising only a single jump (or two perhaps) by two or three notches instead of one will keep your horse on his toes while still keeping the basic exercise from becoming excessively challenging.

TONY'S ADVICE

"This gymnastic teaches your horse a lot about maintaining proper balance in combinations and related lines. It also helps you learn to remain quiet and in perfect balance with your horse."

Setup

Following the diagram, build an oxer at A, followed 57 ft. (17.4m) farther by a vertical at B. Finish by measuring 64 ft. (19.5m) to a final oxer at C.

Set small to moderate-sized jumps that are appropriate to your current level. Have extra ground lines available for reversing the direction of this line.

Benefits

This is an exercise that provides lots of practice in jumping from different stride lengths and influencing your horse's impulsion immediately before and after a jump.

It helps you develop:

▶ timing
▶ control
▶ finesse in executing downward-to-upward transitions and vice versa within the same gait.

It also encourages you to use a shorter release when preparing to compress your horse's stride and will help you develop a correct automatic release.

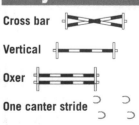

Cross bar

Vertical

Oxer

One canter stride

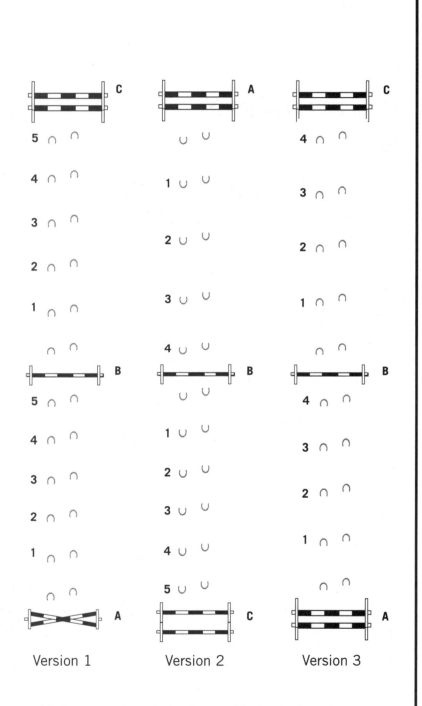

Version 1   Version 2   Version 3

All three versions to be jumped in both directions according to instructions.

RIDING LINES WITH OPTIONAL DISTANCES
A Guest Exercise with Missy Clark

Missy Clark, one of the foremost trainers on the American "A" circuit, offers this final set of exercises for fine tuning your feel and learning to handle one line in a variety of different ways.

How do I ride this?

Version 1

1. Start simple. Have your ground person change oxer A into a cross bar by dropping opposite ends of the front and back poles to the ground.

2. Trot the approach to the cross bar, landing to canter a quiet five strides to the vertical, followed by another quiet five strides to the final oxer at C.

3. Reverse the direction of the pattern. Canter the approach to C quietly, riding for five strides to the vertical, and fitting in a very short five strides to the cross bar at A.

Executing this pattern from C to A is not easy and may require that a novice rider be mounted on an experienced horse.

Version 2

This version is valuable for teaching an inexperienced jumper rider about the added stride.

1. First, reset the oxer at A.

2. Canter the approach to A.

3. Ride a patient four strides to B, followed by a very steady five strides to C.

4. Reverse the direction, this time riding a short five strides from C to B and the steady four strides to A.

Version 3

1. Canter into the oxer at A, keeping the stride compressed but ensuring that you build impulsion as your horse takes the four strides to B.

2. Landing strongly over B, continue in a forward four strides to the final oxer at C.

3. Reverse direction.

4. This time, ride strongly into C so your horse takes four forward strides to B, followed by a steady four to A.

Your horse's open stride must get you to B easily enough that the final strides contain less power than the first ones. If your horse powers over or reaches for the vertical jump at B, he will have difficulty fitting in four comfortable strides in the following distance.

5. Properly done, your horse will quietly land close to the base of the vertical, leaving him plenty of room to fit in the steady four strides to the last oxer.

MISSY'S REMINDER

"This last version is the most difficult; not for beginners. The horse and rider that can effectively and smoothly execute every variation of this exercise is ready for serious competition."

Hap Hansen on Juniperus.

GUEST CONTRIBUTORS

Missy Clark

Having trained or co-trained a national champion at the American Horse Show Association (now USA Equestrian, Inc.) Medal Finals, the ASPCA Maclay Finals, and the East Coast United States Equestrian Team Finals for the last nine years, Missy Clark is known as one of the top trainers of Junior Equitation riders in the United States. She rode and competed herself, working with George Morris and Rodney Jenkins, but stopped showing to devote herself to teaching.

"My true interest lies in the Jumper ring," she says. Among her students are numerous Grand Prix competitors, the Gold Medallist in the 2002 North American Young Riders championship, and the winning members of the national Junior Jumping team in the Prix de States competition at the Pennsylvania National Horse Show.

Anthony D'Ambrosio

Anthony D'Ambrosio won his first Show Jumping competition at the age of nine, then went on to set the indoor world record on Sympatico, jumping 7 feet, 4 inches in 1973. He surpassed that ten years later by jumping 7 feet, 7½ inches on Sweet 'n Low, a record that still stands. He has represented the United States in International competitions many times. He now trains and brings along young horses, as well as designing show jumping courses throughout the United States. His book, *Schooling to Show: Basics of Hunter-Jumper Training* (Viking Press, 1978), is a classic.

Anthony D'Ambrosio

Joe Fargis

"It is important to remember that our horses are living, breathing, thinking, and feeling creatures," says Joe Fargis. "We must treat them that way — as we would each other or a child — with a combination of firmness and kindness. Never surprise your horse. Make sure you are consistent and quiet with your aids. Don't get mad at your horse when *you* have made the mistake."

Kindness and consistency, coupled with quiet basics and flawless form, are keys to Joe Fargis's riding and training style and part of the philosophy that has made him one of the greatest riders in Show Jumping history. Winning 1984 Olympic Gold Medals in the Individual and Team Show Jumping with only one rail down out of 91 obstacles jumped remains an Olympic record. Gold in the 1987 Pan Am Games and Silver in the 1988 Olympics are only two of his many prizes.

Joe first represented the United States in International competition in 1970, where he helped seal the win for the USA in his first Nations Cup appearance. He was also a member of the Gold Medal team at the 1975 Pan American Games and has ridden on numerous Nations Cups teams all over the world.

Still actively competing at the Grand Prix and International levels, Joe also coaches a small group of students and conducts riding clinics throughout the United States.

Hap Hansen

California's Hap Hansen is the most winning U.S. rider ever in the history of the sport of Show Jumping and the first rider to surpass the two million dollar mark in career earnings.

Among his awards are the Rolex Crown of Excellence, the National Grand Prix League (NGL) Western Conference Rider of the Year, the Rolex/NGL Western Conference Rider of the Year, and the AHSA Hertz Equestrian of the Year. He has been a perennial leading rider at the Spruce Meadows Classic in Canada and has represented the United States in International competition many times.

Hap freely credits his great horses for his success and is renowned for his sportsmanship and helpfulness to other competitors.

James Wofford

"I am lucky to have been surrounded throughout my life by horses of all shapes, sizes, and abilities, and from each one who has passed through my life, I have learned something. That process continues today." So says Olympian Jimmy Wofford, a mainstay of the United States Equestrian Team's Three-day Event squad for two decades. Named to four Olympic teams, he rode to two team Silver medals and was awarded four National Championships, along with earning an Individual Silver at the 1980 alternate Olympics and an Individual World Championship Bronze medal.

Jimmy is now an active coach and trainer and includes among his students 2000 Olympic Gold Medallist David O'Connor and his wife, fellow Silver medal team member Karen O'Connor.

Jim Wofford, Individual Silver Medal winner at the Fountainbleu Alternate Olympics, 1980.

GLOSSARY

Anticipation. Refers to a horse's or rider's tension or anxiety prior to a specific action such as a jump, lead change, or turn. Preparation for an upcoming maneuver is important; however, unplanned or premature changes in balance or position can jeopardize correct execution.

Approach. The way horse and rider get to a jump. An approach can be long or short, from a turn or at an angle, and executed in a variety of different gaits or stride lengths. The quality of the approach directly affects the jumping effort itself.

ASTM/SEI. The two organizations responsible for the helmet safety standard as well as standards in many other industries. ASTM (American Standard for Testing Materials) researches and develops the standard for safety and manufacturing protocol. SEI (Safety Equipment Institute) tests helmets and audits manufacturing facilities to assure they meet the standards. Certified helmets are marked by the logos of both organizations along with the number and year of the standard used.

Automatic release (following hand). The rider's hand over the jump maintains an independent, soft, following contact, resulting in a straight line from elbow to wrist through the reins to the horse's mouth. This independent position is the epitome of the correct advanced jumping position.

Bascule. The arc that a horse's body follows over a fence when he jumps. The correct bascule consists of a smooth arc from poll to tail, with the highest point over the center of the fence. Take-off and landing are equidistant from the fence.

Bending. When the horse's body bends around the rider's inside leg, which is on the girth, while the outside leg is slightly behind the girth, controlling the hindquarters. Bending exercises help develop flexibility; a flexible balanced horse will be able to execute faster turns and smoother jumps.

Bulge. When a horse drifts off the track of a circle or part of a circle to the outside. Often results from poor response to the leg aid or the horse turning its head and neck in the correct direction while the rest of its body does not follow.

Cavalletti. The traditional name for elevated trotting or ground poles; can refer to the individual pole with supports on the ends, or to a line of trotting poles, or to a complete exercise including trot poles plus various obstacles in a line.

Chip, Chip-in. When a horse takes an extra, very short stride just before jumping in order to get closer to the fence. Often a horse will chip-in to regain balance when the rider has tipped forward at the last minute. Horses also chip when they feel it is safer than jumping from an exceptionally long distance.

Closing circle (opening circle). Circling after the final fence (or going through the finish) on a course. Used in training to assure the horse remains obedient and concentrates throughout the exercise, including after the final jumping effort.

Counter-canter (canter on the counter lead). A training exercise in which the horse leads with the outside foreleg maintaining a corresponding bend in its body, while executing a smooth turn in the opposite direction.

Crest release. Used in beginning and intermediate jumping, the rider presses his hands forward and down on the horse's crest to stabilize his upper body during a jump. For beginning riders, this can include pinching the mane for greater security. A long crest release requires releasing all contact with the horse's mouth, while a short release maintains contact to some degree.

Cross bar (cross rail, X-bar). A simple jump consisting of two jump poles, with opposite ends of each placed in jump cups and the other ends resting on the ground to create an "X." Often used as a warm-up jump, or the first obstacle of a gymnastic.

Cross-canter. See **Disunited**.

Cut-in. When a horse cuts to the inside of any part of a circle, usually by leaning to the inside of the turn or not bending in the shape of the circle's arc.

Distance. 1) Describes the measured or relative distance between two obstacles: "Jump #1 to #2 is set on a 60' (18.20 m) distance," or "The short distance in the double combination means my horse will have to compress his stride while jumping it."
2) The process of the horse and rider "seeing" (i.e. recognizing in advance) how the current stride will present the horse to the jump.
3) The measured length of a complete jumping course.

Disunited (cross-cantering). Cantering with one leg leading in front and the opposite leg leading in back. Somewhat uncomfortable for horse and rider alike; horses not consistent in executing "flying lead changes" often change the front lead only, leaving themselves disunited.

"Ducking." An exaggerated and quick movement of the rider's upper body forward or down on the horse's neck as the horse jumps. Although various size jumps require the rider's position to accommodate the horse's jumping effort, the rider should endeavor to remain smooth and balanced. A secure leg creates a base of support that will permit the rider to remain over the balance point of his horse throughout the jump with only subtle changes in upper body position.

Fédération Equestre Internationale (FEI). The international governing body for equestrian sports.

Flying change of lead. During the suspension phase of a canter or gallop stride, the horse switches from one leading leg to the other. See **Leads.**

Focal point. A specific point to which a rider is directing the horse; usually something at the perimeter of the arena that riders can use to determine if they are indeed on a straight line.

Focus. A calm and directed concentration on the task at hand; permits the rider to be precise and accurate in communicating with the horse while riding and jumping. The ability to focus on the correct track, pace, and balance produces effective riding. Learning to keep one's focus a suitable distance beyond the current position is critical to riding complex jumping courses accurately.

Following hand. The primary release for advanced jumping riders. The rider's hand follows the horse's mouth over the jumps, always maintaining a light contact and straight line from elbow to wrist to bit.

Full-seat. The weight of the upper body is carried in the saddle through a supple yet straight and nearly vertical back. The ultimate use of the full-seat is in pure dressage.

Getting ahead. Riders are considered to have gotten ahead of the horse when they shift their balance or position forward prior to their horse actually pushing off the ground at the jump. The more extreme version is often referred to as "jumping ahead" and can result in a horse that "chips" (adds a short, last-second stride immediately before take-off) or refuses.

Grid. A series of poles and/or jumps, generally in a straight line.

Grob (or Sunken Road/Devil's Dyke). A combination jump consisting of a slope down to a ditch and a rise back up. There may be a jump going in, followed by either one or two strides to the ditch (with or without a jump over it) and one or two strides up, with or without another jump at the top.

Ground line. A line created by a pole, flower box, small wall, or loose brush that defines the base of a jump on the take-off side. Used to encourage the horse to place his take-off point further back from the base of the jump and to remind a less experienced horse to fold his front legs earlier.

Gymnastic. The general term for a specific exercise in which a pattern of multiple obstacles is used to practice a series of jumps and striding that relate them one to another.

Half-seat (two point or galloping position). Puts 100 percent of the rider's weight into the leg so the seat is entirely clear of the saddle. The most extreme example is flat-racing jockeys, followed by steeplechase jockeys.

Leads. At the canter or gallop, the correct leading leg (on a circle, the inside fore and hind will be placed well ahead of the outside) will permit the horse to remain balanced around turns. A change in direction normally requires a change of lead. See **Flying change, Simple change, Counter canter, Disunited.**

Left behind. Falling behind the motion of the horse's jump; this is the opposite of getting ahead. Provided the rider does not allow his or her hands to rise or otherwise put pressure on the horse's mouth, being slightly behind the horse off the ground rarely bothers the horse very much. However, it feels awkward to the rider, and often results in the rider getting ahead at a future fence in an effort to remedy the problem.

Lengthened stride. A stride length at any gait longer than the horse's medium stride that maintains balance, energy, and rhythm.

Light-seat. The basic and most frequently used position for jumping. The rider's weight is distributed primarily along the legs, sinking through non-rigid hips, knees, and ankles into the heels, while the the front portion of the seat bones maintain light contact with the saddle.

Lip of the cup. The top edge of the jump cup, furthest from the take-off side of the obstacle. Balancing one or both ends of a pole on the lip of the cup can be an alternative should safety cups or shallow jump cups not be available. Especially for the back pole of oxers and other spreads, this can prevent any loss of balance for a horse should he misjudge the width of a jump. If the back pole is secured too tightly, it could prevent the horse from freeing his front legs to facilitate his landing during an awkward effort.

Liverpool. A water ditch with rails over it. The jump itself may be a vertical, an oxer, or a triple bar. A rubber or plastic "tray" with water in it on top of the ground is sometimes substituted for a real ditch.

Loose. Refers to a rider's insecurity in the saddle when the horse jumps or moves quickly. Also, horses are sometimes referred to as being "loose with their front legs" when their technique over the jump does not include tightly folding the lower legs.

Medium trot (or canter). For purposes of schooling for jumping, a gait that is neither lethargic nor hurried or tense. Strides should be of a medium length, with the horse balanced to be able to immediately and instantly either lengthen or shorten his stride.

Off-stride. Meeting a jump in a manner that will require the horse to make a last-second adjustment to his stride length in order to create an appropriate take-off point for the jump.

Opening circle (closing circle). The initial circle ridden prior to approaching the first jump of a course. Usually, but not always, begun at the trot, it is used to establish the appropriate rhythm and pace before jumping.

Out of stride. Describes a jump that is met smoothly with no change or adjustment in the horse's stride before take-off or after landing.

Over-jumping. When a horse gives an unnecessarily extraordinary effort over a fence. Usually done by a green horse just learning to jump or by a horse jumping a new or unusually spooky fence for the first time.

Oxer. A spread jump with a front (the take-off side of the obstacle) and a back (landing side) element that are constructed either to be equal in height or with the front element slightly lower than the back. Normally only a single pole (never a plank, gate, or wall) is used for the back element.

Pace. A general term indicating the combination of gait, speed, stride, and energy that a horse is using in negotiating a jumping course.

Placing pole. A single pole placed on the approach to a jump, or occasionally following the landing, to aid in creating the desired point of take-off or to regulate the strides on the approach or departure from a jump.

Quick. Describes a horse that hurries the take-off at the jump; often resulting in a flat arc or bascule over the jump and/or a speedy, erratic, or tense attitude toward the jumping course.

Refusal. When a horse approaches the jump but fails to make a jumping effort. A horse might refuse some distance from the jump or immediately before take-off.

Rhythm. Maintaining rhythm indicates a horse that is not changing speed within a gait but proceeding forward with a regular and consistent tempo. The rider has a direct influence on the horse's ability to achieve, maintain, or regain a good rhythm.

Rub or rubbing (as in rubbing the pole). Describes a horse touching the fence without knocking it down.

Run-out. Describes a horse evading the taking of a jump by going to the side of it.

Safety cups. First developed in 1993, they are designed and carefully manufactured to release when a horse delivers approximately 135 kilos of downward pressure. This allows the jump pole to fall free. Safety cups are mandatory in competitions sanctioned by the Fédération Equestre Internationale. Their use has all but eliminated the fall of horses in today's show jumping at that level.

Schoolmaster. An experienced older horse or pony whose job now is to teach inexperienced riders.

Scooting. When the horse moves off quickly and unexpectedly, often leaving the rider behind his motion. Can be a result of a spook or just a fresh and overly playful attitude.

Shortened stride. A stride length at any gait that is shorter than a horse's medium stride and maintains balance, energy, and rhythm.

Simple change of lead. When the lead change is executed through a precise transition of 2 to 4 strides of either a walk or trot before resuming the canter on the opposite lead. See **Leads.**

Slow (in front or behind). Describes a horse that does not raise or fold the legs quickly enough to avoid rubbing the jump. A horse that does not fold up one or both front legs — by raising the shoulder towards the horizontal and bending the knee and fetlock joints — is said to be "hanging."

Spread. A jump that involves width as well as height. Generally the width will be set slightly more than the respective height of a given obstacle.

Square halt. A halt where the horse's weight is evenly distributed on all four legs while standing immobile. A correct halt is always square.

Standards (wing, upright, stick, or simple). Hold the jump cups that support the ends of poles. Wing standards are usually approximately 24 to 30 inches (60 to 75 cm) wide. Simple (also referred to as stick or upright) standards are constructed with a simple upright (5 to 6 feet or 1.50 to 1.80 m tall) mounted on a base or foot.

Track. The specific line to be followed between jumps on a course. The track includes the approach to the first jump (often including a preparatory circle) and the finish to the exercise or course after the final jump. Determining the most appropriate track is a very important part of preparing for show jumping, equitation, and eventing courses. Walking the course prior to riding it provides an opportunity to analyze the course in detail prior to a competition.

The ability to execute the track accurately is a function of training and level of communication between horse and rider, as well the as focus and concentration of each.

Transition. The change from one gait to another, or from one length of stride to another. Upward transitions are those from slower to faster (i.e. walk to trot, or medium canter to canter on a lengthened stride), while downward transitions are those from faster to slower (i.e. trot to halt or medium trot to trot on a shortened stride).

Trot grid. A set of three to four ground poles placed so the horse takes one stride over each pole at the trot; often used to indicate the approach and take-off point for the initial jump of a gymnastic line.

Two-point (half seat or galloping position). Puts 100 percent of the rider's weight into the leg, permitting the seat to be entirely clear of the saddle; used in training to secure and strengthen the leg position, as well as for times in competition when a total freedom from weight on the horse's back is desirable.

Vertical. A jump that involves height without width; vertical jumps can consist of poles, gates, planks, or walls, alone or in combination.

Visualization. A valuable sports psychology technique in which the rider will complete a mental review of every aspect of an exercise or course prior to actually executing it. This technique can be extremely helpful, especially when the rider mentally "feels" the approach and departure to the jumps, including the turns and changes of pace, not simply the jumps themselves.

Wait/Waiting. When jumping, waiting means not anticipating or signaling in any way for the horse to jump. Rather, the rider waits for the horse to focus on the job at hand without hurrying or rushing to or over the jump.

ANNOTATED BIBLIOGRAPHY

This is only a selection of the best books on training jumpers! Starting your library with these will give you a head start in your equestrian education.

D'Endrody, Lt. Col. A.L. *Give Your Horse a Chance*. London: JA Allen, 1989 (1999). A classic book, with excellent sections on training and conditioning the jumper and event horse.

De Nemethy, Bertlan. *The De Nemethy Method*. New York: Doubleday & Co., 1988 (1999). As USET Show Jumping coach from 1952–1984, De Nemethy molded the American Jumping Style and took it to its peak. A must for every library.

Harris, Susan E. *The United States Pony Club Manuals of Horsemanship*. New York: Howell Book House
   The United States Pony Club Manuals of Horsemanship — Basics for Beginners D Level, 1994.
      The United States Pony Club Manuals of Horsemanship — Intermediate Horsemanship C Level, 1995.
      The United States Pony Club Manuals of Horsemanship — Horsemanship B, HA, A Levels, 1996.
Thorough and full of excellent information. Even the lowest levels are fairly advanced.

Jackson, Noel. *Effective Horsemanship*. New York: Arco Publishing, 1967. An older (and out-of-print) book that has a lot of excellent information about jumping and training the jumping horse.

Chapot, Frank with Arlene J. Newman. *Winning with Frank Chapot*. New York: Breakthrough Publications, 1992. Chapot, now coach of the United States Olympic Show Jumping Team, is one of America's greats, and this book has lots of good information.

D'Ambrosio, Anthony. *Schooling to Show: Basics of Hunter-Jumper Training*. New York: Doubleday & Co., 1978. Another wonderful book of basics that is sadly out of print.

Kursinski, Anne. *Anne Kursinski's Riding and Jumping Clinic*. New York: Doubleday & Co., 1995. Anne grew up under the tutelage of the late Jimmy Williams, then moved to George Morris. She is classic in her approach and explains things well.

Klimke, Ingrid and Reiner. *Cavalletti* (revised edition). London: JA Allen, 2000. Another excellent book on gymnastics and cavalletti work.

Littauer, Vladimer S. *The Forward Seat.* New York: Derrydale Press, 1937. One of the early proponents of the forward seat here in America, and one of the first books on the subject.

Morris, George. *Hunter Seat Equitation.* New York: Doubleday & Co., 1990. An absolute must-have from "God" of the H/J world.
  Hunter Seat Equitation. The American Jumping Style. New York: Doubleday & Co., 1993. An excellent analysis of the American as well as European Jumping styles.

O'Connell, Alice L. *Pamela and the Blue Mare.* Boston: Putnam, 1952.
  The Blue Mare in the Olympic Trials. Boston: Putnam, 1956.
These two little novels detail the training of a horse from ground up. Dressage, gymnastic jumping, and cross country riding are all covered and very understandable. Does your child/student not really understand gymnastics and the importance of flatwork? This explains it all and tells a lovely story as well. Vladimer Littauer and Col Wofford (Jimmy Wofford's father, an Olympian in his own right) were the technical advisors for these novels.

Richter, Judy. *Horse & Rider.* New York: Doubleday & Co., 1984. Judy, a graduate "A" Pony Clubber, is a veteran trainer on the top show circuit, and has been called one of the best teachers in the business.

An English teacher before becoming a full-time professional, she has written a clear and easy-to-use basic manual.

Steinkraus, William, *Riding and Jumping.* New York: Doubleday & Co., 1969. A book of riding and philosophy from the 1968 Gold Medal winner. Another must-read, along with its sequel, *Reflections on Riding and Jumping* (Trafalgar Square, 1991).

Wofford, James, *Training the Three-Day Event Horse and Rider.* New York: Doubleday Equestrian Library, 1995. NOT just for the event horse and rider! Excellent exercises presented in an easy format. Lots of discussion of fitness and flatwork — both essential for any jumping.
  Gymnastics: Systematic Training for Jumping Horses. Warwickshire, GB: Compass Books, 2001. Hard to find in the United States, this is another excellent little gymnastics book.

Wright, Gordon. *Learning to Ride, Show and Hunt.* New York: Doubleday & Co., 1966. A classic in the field! Mr. Wright was George Morris's teacher and mentor.

In most countries, there are excellent weekly and monthly periodicals offering ongoing articles on training that may be helpful.

Also, keep your eyes open for clinics and educational symposiums by top trainers in your area.

INDEX

Linda Allen on Union Jack.

OTHER STOREY TITLES YOU MIGHT ENJOY

101 Arena Exercises by Cherry Hill. Suitable for both English and Western riders, this classic, best-selling equestrian workbook presents both traditional and original exercises, patterns, and maneuvers. Can be hung on the wall or on an arena fence for easy reference. 224 pages. Paperback with comb binding. ISBN 0-88266-316-X.

101 Horsemanship & Equitation Patterns by Cherry Hill. This sequel to *101 Arena Exercises* (above) is a compendium of the essential patterns for Western Horsemanship and English Equitation competition. 256 pages. Paperback with comb binding. ISBN 1-58017-159-1.

The Horse Doctor Is In by Brent Kelley. Combining solid veterinary advice with enlightening stories from his Kentucky equine practice, Dr. Kelley informs readers on all aspects of horse health care from fertility to fractures to foot care. 416 pages. ISBN 1-58017-460-4 (paperback); ISBN 1-58017-430-2 (hardcover).

Horse Handling and Grooming by Cherry Hill. This user-friendly guide to essential skills includes feeding, haltering, tying, grooming, clipping, bathing, braiding, and blanketing. The wealth of practical advice offered is thorough enough for beginners, yet useful for experienced riders improving or expanding their horse skills. 160 pages. Paperback. ISBN 0-88266-956-7.

Horse Health Care by Cherry Hill. Explains bandaging, giving shots, examining teeth, deworming, and preventive care. Exercising and cooling down, hoof care, and tending wounds are depicted, along with taking a horse's temperature and determining pulse and respiration rates. 160 pages. Paperback. ISBN 0-88266-955-9.

Horsekeeping on a Small Acreage by Cherry Hill. The essentials for designing safe and functional facilities, whether you have one acre or one hundred. 192 pages. Paperback. ISBN 0-88266-596-0.

Storey's Guide to Raising Horses by Heather Smith Thomas. A comprehensive guide facilities, feeding and nutrition, daily health care, disease prevention, foot care, dental care, selecting breeding stock, foaling, and care of the young horse. 512 pages. Paperback. ISBN 1-58017-127-3.

Storey's Horse Lover's Encyclopedia edited by Deborah Burns. This hefty, fully illustrated, comprehensive A-to-Z compendium is an indispensable answer book addressing every question a reader may have about horses and horse care. 480 pages. ISBN 1-58017-317-9 (paperback); ISBN 1-58017-336-5 (hardcover).

These books and other Storey books are available at your bookstore, tack store, farm store, garden center, or directly from Storey Books, 210 MASS MoCA Way, North Adams, MA 01247, or by calling 1-800-441-5700. Or visit our Web site at www.storey.com.